COOKE EDGAR D COOKE DEREK J. C. COOKSON TOM COOLEN JEAN M COOLEY DR GORDEN COOMBS MATTHEW COOMBS STANLEY COOMBS BARRY COOPER BIRGIT COOPER CLAUDIA
COOPER GARY COOPER GLENN K COOPER JOHN R. COOPER MAVIS COOPER MICHAEL COOPER ROBERT G. COOPER ROBERT H. COOPER RON COOPER RONALD E COOPER JAMES COOTE
JOHN E. COPELAND JUNE N. COPELAND LEONARD COPELAND KENNETH CORBETT JOCELYNE CORBIN ROBERT J CORBIN TERENCE CORBITT MARY CORCORAN-CREWE ALBERT J.
CORCORAN CLIFTON CORCORAN DAVID CORCORAN PETER W. CORISH JOHN CORKERY CHARLOTTE CORMIER CHRIS CORMIER DONNA CO CORMIER GLEN CORMIER
JAMES CORMIER M BRUCE CORMIER REGIS JOSEPH CORMIER ROBERT CORMIER ROBERT CORMIER VALENTIN CORNEA JORGE CLARENCE M COSTELLO
CHARLES J. COTE GUY COTE NORMAN L. COTTEE SYLVIA COTTOM GEORGE COTTON RAYNALD COTTON ALEX C. COU Y COURT DAVID COURTE
DEVIN COURTE TYRONE COURTE RUTH THOMAS COURTNEY ERNIE COURTOREILLE LEONA J. COURTOREILLE R OURVOISIER ROBERT COUSINS
HENRY COUTURE JACKSON J.W. COUTURE JACQUES COUTURE REAL COUTURE GREG COUTURIER BRIAN COVE NE A COWAN JULIAN COWARD JEFFREY
COWIE ROGER COWLES JAMES R COX JANICE COX MIKE J CRAGGS ANNE CRANE BOB CRANE FRANK E. CRANE D ANTHONY CRAVEN CATHERINE CRAWFORD ELDON
CRAWFORD PEGGY CRAWFORD DAVID CREWE REGINALD A CREWE BRENDA CRICKMORE TIMOTHY CRILLY BRUCE CRISBY GLYNN CRISBY PATRICK CRISBY RAYFIELD CRISBY TODD
CRITCH PATRICK G CRITCHELL GAYLE CROCKER RONALD C. CROCKFORD BRIAN CRONIN CORNELIUS CRONIN GREG CROSLAND CLAUDE S. CROSS HENRY CROSS HUGH CROSS MARK
CROSS MARVEY JOHN CROSS FRANK CROSSLEY DENNIS CROUCHER ROBERT CROUCHER DAVID CROWE GARRY G. CROWE BRENDA CROWTHER CAROL CROWTHER DOUGLAS O.
CROWTHER MICHAEL B. CROWTHER PAUL CROWTHER CHRISTOPHER CROZIER MARTIN K CRUMMY GRAHAM CUDDY RAMSAY CUFF J. RUSSEL CUKR RANDY CULL WILSON CULL
CLAUDE CULLIHALL GRENVILLE CULLIHALL JOHN G. CULLITON ALEX CUMBERLAND BARRY G CUMMINGS BRUCE CUMMINGS RAYMOND E. CUMMINGS HEATHER CUNNINGHAM
MURRAY CUNNINGHAM SHERRI-ANN CURR DANIEL CURRAN DAVID J. CURRAN ROBERT CURRIE LIONEL CUTLER WILSON CUTLER LUBOMYR M. O. CYMBALISTY GEORGE J.
CYMERMAN PAUL CYPRIEN RITA CYPRIEN LEO L. CYR KRZYSZTOF CZAJEWSKI AUGUSTO S D'ALMEIDA HEATHER D'ARNE OSMOND J. D'CUNHA SURESH A. D'LIMA ADRIAN D'SILVA
BARRY D'SILVA NIKKI D'SILVA RICHARD J. D'SILVA SIMON D'SILVA QAIS K. DABBAGH ALFRED P DAHL TONY S. DAI AMY DAKIN BLAIR DAKIN COLIN C. DAKIN LEO P DAKIN PETER DAKIN
ROGER DAKIN MICHAEL S. DALEY PETER DALEY PATRICIA J DALK MICHAEL R. DALTON ARTHUR DALY JOHN DALY PATRICK DALY JAMES E. DALZIEL LAURIE DANIELSON MICHEL J.
DANIS TODD DANSON TRENT DANSON WALTER DANSON LILLIAN DARICHUK DARCY DAUGELA VALERIE L DAUPHINEE GERALD DAVENPORT PATRICIA DAVEY PETER DAVEY C. VICTOR
DAVIES DONNA M DAVIES GEORGE DAVIES STEPHEN DAVIES STEPHEN T. DAVIES TUDOR DAVIES VIVEEN DAVIES AKEELA DAVIS EDWARD DAVIS ERIC DAVIS GERALD D. DAVIS GLENN
DAVIS GREGORY R. DAVIS HARDY J. DAVIS JOHN DAVIS JOHN J. DAVIS MICHAEL DAVIS PAUL DAVIS RANDALL DAVIS THOMAS DAVIS YVONNE DAVISON JAMES M. DAWSON DONALD
DAY PATRICK DAY DAVE B. DAYE CHARLES DE CARO DENISE DE CRESCENTIS DON DE GUERRE FREDERIK R DE HAAS ANDRIES DE JONG ARMANDO S DE LA CRUZ ARTHUR DE LINT
DINO J. DE MARTIN BINAY K DE TODD W. DEAN VICTOR DEAN WILLIAM DEAN REG W DEARING BERT DEARMOND KENNETH EARL DEARY JASPER DECKER KEVIN DECKER NICK DEEG
PATSY B DEEP THOMAS E DEEVY BRENT DEFREITAS ADELARD A DEGAGNE PATRICK DEHAAS ERLINDA DELA-CRUZ EVAN J. DELEFF ROBERT DELISLE CLAUDIO DELLAMAESTRA MARIO
H DELOS REYES JOHN DELOYER MAXIMO DELUSONG ROCH DEMERS JAMES DEMMONS THOMAS DEMOREST ALLAN DENEVE BRIGITTE DENEVE ADELARD J. DENIS DONALD DENNEY
SCOTT DENNIS WILLIAM L DENNIS RODNEY DENTON BRIAN DENYER LARRY DENYER ROGER M DERASP GORDON DERKSON RICARDO J. DERMO BRENT DEROCHIE KEN DERPACK
ALBERT DERY MIKE J DESEGUIN REAL DESJARDINS ANTHONY G DESJARLAIS RICHARD DESJARLAIS SHANNON DESJARLAIS JOHN DEVASSY CLIFFORD DEVEAU JACQUELINE
DEVENNE RICHARD DEVENNE SEAN DEVINE JOHN DEVISON PETER C DEVLIN DAVE L. DEWEY MONTE DEWEY ALOK DEY PERRY DHILLON LESLIE T. DIACHINSKY ALAIN DIALLO ALBERT
DICKS JEFF DICKS LEONARD DICKS DONALD DICKSON TERRENCE DICKSON LAURENCE E J DIERKENS DONALD CHARLES DIETRICH JOSEPH N. DIFABIO BRIAN DIGGORY JOHN DILLON
PAUL F DILLON CHRISTIAN C DIONNE DOREEN DIONNE KAREN DIONNE LAWRENCE R DIPASQUALE JOHN T. DISCHER CRAIG DITTRICH ROSS A. DIXON DAN DIZAK ARTO DJERDJERIAN
SVEN G DJURFORS DAVE DMYTRIW RANJIT S DOAD THOMAS A. DOBBIE BRIAN B DOBBS MARY DOBBS ALLAN M DOBLANKO WILLIAM J. DOCHSTADER TERRY DODGE EFFIE R
DODIGOVICH ROBERT DODYK HANS DOERTH BARRY DOHERTY LORNA DOHERTY ROBERT DOHERTY FRANK N. DOLLING VICTOR DOLLMAN DANNY DOMINGUE DONALD A DOMINGUE
MAREK DOMINSKI JAMES A. DON JAMES R. DON JR. DAVE DONALD DOUGLAS DONALD GERALD WILLIAM DONNELLY LINDA DONNELLY GLENDA DONOVAN-MALIK CATHERINE V
DOODY GLENN DOONANCO J. D. DORAN JAMES A DORIE JEANNE DORIE PETER DOUCET ROBERT DOUCET MICHAEL W. DOUCETTE ROLAND A. DOUCETTE PATRICK D DOUGAN
KENNETH DOUGLAS BRUCE DOW DEBORAH DOWDEN BERTRAM DOWNER JAMES M DOWNEY JOSEPH P DOWNEY MARTIN J. DOWNEY NATHAN G DOWNEY ROBERT DOWNEY STEVE
DOWNEY JED DOWNIE DORMAN DOYLE HUGH DOYLE MICHEL DOYLE NORMAND DOYLE CATHERINE DRAGON WILLIAM DRANE ALBERTO J. DRANSUTAVICIUS PATRICK DREADDY
FELIX DROVER AUBREY DRUGGETT DONALD DRUMMOND ADRIEN DUBE JOHN H. DUBEAU LEO DUBECK LIONEL A. DUBOIS ROBERT DUCHARME KEN DUDDLE NEVILLE C. DUFF
BRENDAN F DUFFY JOSEPH DUFFY THOMAS E. DUFFY CYRIL J. DUGGAN PETER DUGGAN IAN G. DUNCAN EGILS DUNENS PETER B. DUNFIELD DIANE DUNN GORDON DUNN MICHAEL
F DUNN PAUL JOSEPH DUNPHY RAYMOND DUNPHY DAVID DUNSWORTH CLAUDE DUPUIS GILLES G. DURAND WILLIAM DURNO CLARENCE DUROCHER ERNEST J DUROCHER JAMES
DUROCHER ROBERT DURRANT KATALIN DUSEK PETER E DUSEK LES L. DUSYK VIVIAN DUSYK PATRICIA A. DUTCHAK DOREEN DUTKA JAMES J. DUTTON HARRY DVORSKY LEO C DWYER
PATRICK DWYER ROBERT DWYER LUBOMIR DZURILLA DONALD I. EARLE GEORGE B. EASTMAN LOIS EASTON IVAN EATON KENNETH EBERHARDT DARRIN J. ECKEL EDWARD ECKES
ABBIE R. EDDY ALEC R. EDDY CHRISTOPHER B. EDDY CORINNE EDDY JIM EDDY KEVIN EDDY PAULA EDDY PHYLLIS EDDY RANDALL EDGAR HOWARD EDMUNDS JEAN EDMUNDS JOHN
EDMUNDS LYNNE EDMUNDS RONALD EDMUNDS TERRY A EDMUNDS JOSEPH EDWARDS FREDERICK EEFTING CYRIL EFFORD MARGARET EGAN KENNETH EHRY ROSALIND EICHHORN
MOHAMED EL-HAYOUNI DOUG ELGIE ALEXANDER ELIEFF MICHAEL ELIUK WALTER ELIUK KURT ELKJAR CALVYN R. ELLERTON CARL R ELLERTON FRED K. ELLERTON JIM A. ELLERTON
JOHN A. ELLINGSEN DEBRA ELLIOT STUART ELLIOT ANDY ELLIOTT DAVID ELLIOTT DAVID ELLIOTT JAMES B ELLIOTT JOHN ELLIOTT KEN ELLIOTT SHARON ELLIOTT HOWARD L. ELLIS
RONALD ELLSWORTH RUSTON ELLSWORTH ROBERT D ELLWOOD DEREK ELSER DAVID W. ELSON G. ELSON PETER F EMSLEY WILLIAM A ENGE FRANK ENNIS BRUNO D. ERELIS JR.
BRUNO SR. ERELIS SHIRLEY ERELIS E.LEIF ERIKSEN GERALD W. ERKER PETER ERL BERNARD ERLINGER-FORD JOHN ERLINGER-FORD KENNETH ERSKINE LYNNE C ERSKINE GEORGE
ESCH ARIS A. ESPEJO PAUL ESPEZEL EDWARD EVANS FRED EVANS LISA EVANS MICHAEL J. EVANS PHILIP J EVANS ROBERT EVANS ANDREW R EVERETT DAWNA EVERETT TODD F.
EVERETT JOANNE EVOY WINSTON EVOY JAMES EXELL JOHN EZEKIEL MIKE EZEKIEL TERRY FACKRELL WILLIAM FADDEN (JR) WILLIAM V FADDEN SR BRUCE FAICHNEY EMMA FAICHNEY
ROGER E FAICHNEY ALAN FAIR BLAIR FAIRLESS EUGENIO (JAY) FALCONE DAVID FAMULAK CARLA FANDRY SHANE L FANDRY JEFF FANNING JOAN FARGEY ANTAL FARKAS KATHY
FARKAS LES FARKAS DAVID FARRELL KENNETH FARRELL WINSTON FARRELL LINDA L FARYNA GARY FARYNIUK DIANE FAULKNER DOUGLAS L. FAULKNER DEREK FAWCETT JAMES
R. FAWCETT MICHAEL A. FAWCETT WESLEY J. FEDEC ANDREW FEDIUK DOREEN FEDORCHUK SANDRA FEDORCHUK AMBROSE FEDORETZ ALLAN M. FEDUN DAVID FEDUN GEORGIA
A FEDYNAK BARBARA FEHR ADOLPH FEINGOLD BRAMWELL L FELTHAM JEFF FELTHAM TONY B FELTHAM DAVE FENNELL KEITH FENTON ERNEST FENTY DAVID FERGUSON JAMES
B. FERGUSON LYNNE FERGUSON WAYNE FERGUSON HENRY FERN DENIS FERNANDES PHILIP MICHAEL FERNANDES ROLAND E FERNANDES JOSE F. FERREIRA LOUIS FERREIRA JIM
R. FERRIS LANCE A. D. FERRISS JAMES FETZKO WILHELM FEXA ROBERT J. FIDDER ROBERT FIDDLER KEITH FIDLER TONY FIFIELD JIM M FIGIEL MICHAEL FIGIEL MICHEL HENRY FILION
WILLIAM FILLATRE NEIL FINDLATER CINDY FINLAY GRANT D FINLAY GLEN FINNSON CAROLE FIRLOTTE GARRY FIRMANIUK WAYNE J. FIRTH BRIAN FISHER CARL D FISHER KRIS FISHER
PETER FISHER ROBERT FISHER THOMAS FITCHETT DAVID FITZGERALD JR. BERNIE FITZGERALD DAVID E. FITZGERALD JOHN T. FITZGERALD PAULETTE FITZGERALD SHARON
FITZGERALD FREDERICK FITZPATRICK KEN FITZPATRICK MICHELLE FITZPATRICK WILLIAM FITZPATRICK DAVID W. FIZZARD DELBERT I. FIZZELL LAURIE FLANDERS GORDON FLASHA
ANTHONY FLEMING DAVID S FLEMING ELLEN FLEMING PAUL FLEMING SELBY FLEMING TODD FLEMING BONNIE L. FLESHER ROY FLETCHER ALLAN M. FLETT CLIFFORD FLETT DONNA
FLETT DOUGLAS FLETT FRAN FLETT GARRY K. FLETT MILDRED J FLETT ROBERT L. FLETT RONALD J. FLETT TIMOTHY G. FLETT JAMES FLEURY MAURICE FLEURY BERNARD N FLIGHT
CRAIG FLIGHT DOUGLAS O FLINT ALBERT FLOOD RALPH L FLOWERS FRANK FLYNN HOWARD J. FLYNN SEAN FLYNN THADDEUS, P FLYNN NORMAN P. FONG JAMES M. FORBES JOHN
FORBES RICHARD G FORBES ART FORBISTER DANIEL FORBISTER LESTER C. FORBISTER GEORGE FORD GLENN FORD JAMES G F FORD MARTIN FORD ELAINE FOREMAN ROBERT A
FORESTER JOHN H. FORSTER ROBERTA FORSTER SHARON FORSTER ANDY G. FORTIER DANNY FORTIER MIKE FORTIER EDWARD J. FORTIN MARY FORTIN STEPHEN FORWARD ANDRE
FOSTER ARTHUR FOSTER KEN FOSTER WENDY FOSTER PERRY FOTTY GERARD FOUGERE CHRISTOPHER P FOWLER DAVID FOWLOW J. DAVID FOX JACKELENE FOX DONALD J. FOY
JOHN FOY RON FOY CLAUDE FRADETTE VAUGHAN J. FRALEIGH SCOTT FRAMPTON ERIC J FRANCE ALMA M FRANCIS WILFRID FRANCIS WILLIAM FRANCIS ANN FRANCOEUR DENIS
FRANCOEUR JOZEF FRANK LOIS FRANK C DAVID FRANKLIN LEONARD FRASER RONALD H FRASER SHIRLEY FRASER WAYNE FRASER WILLIAM FRASER HARLEY G FREDERICKS MARVIN
FREDERICKSON CLYDE FREEMAN JERRY FREEMAN SUSAN FREEMAN ALAN FREER DAN J FREY DENNIS JOSEPH FREZELL BRUCE FRIESEN DONALD R FRIESEN FREDERICK H FRIESEN
HANS E FRIIS STEPHEN FRISE JAMES FROESE JOHN FROESE JULIA FROESE G. ARNOLD FRY GEORGE FRYE RUSSELL A. FRYKAS LOUISE FUCHS ORVAN FUDGE SAMUEL FUDGE STUART
FULFORD LAWRENCE FULKERSON BETTY SUN MAN FUNG MARTIN FUNG STEPHEN FUNK GERARD FUREY PETER FURGALA ANGELA FURTADO CHRISTIE FURTADO KAREN GABLE KEITH
E GABRIEL RICHARD GABRIELSE MICHAEL GADDE ISAAC GAFUR LOUIS GAGNAUX DENIS GAGNE GABRIEL GAGNE YVETTE GAGNE JULIAN R.J. GAGNON MARGARET GAGON
BERNHARD GAIDER TANYA GALE-MACPHERSON BETTY GALLACHER CHARLES GALLACHER LORNE GALLAGHER ANGELA GALLANT PHILIP GALLANT GARY GALLAUGHER WILLIAM G.
GALLINGER ALDO J GALLO THOMAS GALWAY CAROL GAMACHE TODD GAMMON CLIFFORD GANDEY LINDSAY GANDEY RATTAN GARCHA ANJU GARG BRENDA GARRATT GERRY
GARTLAND MICHAEL GARTNER ROBERT W. GARTSHORE ANNETTE GARUK GORDON GARUK JOSEPH J. GARVEY TEENA GASPICH GORDON GAST CARLOTTA GATES IVAN GATES KEVIN
GAUCHER CECIL J. GAUDET DONALD GAUDET GARRY J. GAUDET GEORGE E. GAUDET MARGARET A. GAUDET STEVEN GAUDET WENDY GAUDET HARRY GAULTON MICHAEL GAULTON
MICHELLE GAULTON ROBERT GAULTON ALAIN GAUTHIER ANDRE GAUTHIER DANIEL GAUTHIER DONNA GAUTHIER JULIAN C. GAUTHIER WAYNE E. GAUTHIER BELINDA GAUVREAU
TIMOTHY GAUVREAU RANDY D GAVEL ROBERT ERNEST GAVELIN FRANK GAYDAR ZSOLT GAZDAG GERALD T. GEAR MARGARET DALE GEE NOEL GEE KENNETH GELECH GAETAN
GENEREUX GAETAN-L GENEREUX MERVIN D. GENOE GERALD GENOVESE ERNST J GENTNER BERNARD GEORGE SAMUEL GEORGE SARAMMA GEORGE ELLEN GERBER LOTHAR
GERBER LESLIE GEREIN BILL GERRITS PHILIPP GHAZAL CAROL GHOSH NIRMAL GHOSH PRIYA GHOSH DARREN GIBBS JOHN GIBBS BEATRICE M GIBERSON KEVIN E. GIBSON KATHRYN
GIEBELHAUS BRUCE A. GIFFORD LOUISE A. GIGLIOTTI OSCAR GILBERTSON ELIZABETH GILCHRIST K ELIZABETH GILDNER MELVYN V. GILES PATRICIA GILES JAI S GILL SATPAL S GILL
JOHN GILLARD ARTHUR GILLESPIE DARLENE GILLETT RALPH GILLINGHAM RANCE GILLINGHAM ROY GILLINGHAM DANIEL W. GILLIS DOUGLAS M. GILLIS MICHAEL GILLIS STEVE M
GILLIS WALTER GILLIS GEORGE GILLISS GREF GILLSTROM GARY GIN FERNAND E GINGRAS MARIO G. GIORDANO JERRY GIRARD RONALD GIRVITZ JOANNE GLADU MALCOLM GLADU
CHARLES GLADUE ENNIS GLADUE FLOYD GLADUE GARRY C. GLADUE WESLEY H GLADUE ETHELBERT GLASGOW JACK P. GLAVINE LINDA GLAVINE PETER GLAVINE LARRY GLOWASKY
ERIC J GNYP LLOYD GOETHALS WES GOGAL BARBARA A GOLDEN G WILLIAM GOLDEN MICHAEL GOLDEN WALTER GOLEMBLASKI ANDREW GOLOSKY PATRICIA GOLOSKY VLADIMIR
G. GOLOWIN MURRAY D GOMMERUD BASELIZA G. GONZALES R.T. GONZALES SILVIA GONZALEZ CONNIE M GOODINE DARYL GOODINE JAMES FREDERICK GOODINE VERDELL
GOODINE GORDON C. GOODRIDGE DAVID A GOODWIN JAMES ALFRED GOODWIN BRIAN GOODYEAR DIANNE GOODYEAR RODNEY A E GOODYEAR ALEXANDER G. GORDON DAVID
NEIL GORDON DONALD GORDON DONALD GORDON EDWARD A GORDON GERALD GORDON KENNETH GORDON MARY-JANE GORDON WILLIAM A. GORDON JULENE GORING WALTER
GORSKI KENNETH GOTTSELIG DAN GOULD DAVID GOULD GARNET GOULD GARTH GOULD GERALDINE GOULD LAURIE GOULD JOHN J GOUVEIA ERNEST GOWANS ANTHONY G. GRACE
BRENT GRAF TERRY GRAF ALAN GRAHAM BEVERLEY GRAHAM BRUCE L. GRAHAM JOHN D. GRAHAM L. WILBER GRAHAM STEPHEN GRAHAM ELIZABETH GRANDJAMBE GORDON
GRANDJAMBE JOE B GRANDJAMBE PETER E GRANDJAMBE RICHARD GRANDJAMBE CHRISTOPHER GRANT CHRISTOPHER GRANT DAVID C. GRANT HENRY GRANT WALLACE GRANT
ROBERT M. GRATTON BRENDA GRAVELLE-STRONG ROSS GRAVELLE BEN GRAY DANIEL GRAY G.RONALD GRAY DENNIS GREEN JOAN GREEN JOHN W.W. GREEN RICHARD GREEN
ROSS R GREEN TERENCE M.D. GREEN THOMAS P GREENE BENJAMIN A GREENFIELD ARTHUR GREENHALGH JAMES GREENHALGH CAROLYN GREENWOOD DAVID GREENWOOD MAY
GREENWOOD ROBERT K. GREENWOOD TERRY GREGOIRE THOMAS GREGOROSCHUK SCOTT GREGORY RANDY GRETZAN RAJINDER GREWAL GEOFFREY GRIFFIN THOMAS O. GRIFFIN
BERNARD S. GRIFFITHS GARY GRIFFITHS KEITH T.W. GRIFFITHS HILTRUD GROSSMANN EDWARD G. GROVE GREG GROVES PHILIP J GROVES MICHAEL GRUBLAK WAYNE GRUDEN

MICHEL A GUAY SERGE GUAY YVON GUAY JOHANNES GUDJONSON DIANA GUENETTE JOHN GUENTHER ERROL GUEVARA ELIZABETH GUILBEAU HOWARD R GUILBEAU COLIN
S. GUILDER NUCCIA GUILDER JOHN A. GUILLET MARYANNE GUILLET A. PAUL GULLAGE DAVID GULLAGE RENE K GUNPUTRAV SHAILENDRA GUPTA ATIL GURHAN RICK W. GURSKI
DAVID GUSHUE DEEDRA GUSHUE DONNA GUSHUE EDWARD GUSHUE EDWARD J. GUSHUE GERRY GUSHUE RANDY GUSHUE PAUL GUSHULAK GARY GUY GLYN GYGI KERMIT
A. HAAKONSON MERLYN K. HABERSTOCK LARRY HACKMAN ALAN HADDEN JEFFREY C HADFIELD JAMES HADLEY KENNETH J HAEBERLE MELISSA HAFFEN PAUL HAGAR BARRY
M. HAGEN KEITH HAGEN LAURENCE HAGEN MICHAEL S HAGERMAN PHILIP R HAGERMAN ROSTISLAV (RUSTY) HALAS RONALD HALE JOHN HALEY LEO HALEY GEOFFREY
HALFERDAHL SUSAN I. HALFERDAHL ANNETTE HALL BRYCE HALL CHARLES J. HALL DAVID HALL DAVID A HALL GERVIN D HALL JACK HALL JOSEPH HALL MAUREEN HALL PATRICIA
HALL ROBERT HALL ROBERT H. HALL WESLEY HALL WILLIAM A.H. HALL JOE HALLORAN CAROLYN HAMBLEY KEITH D HAMBLEY DEMETRI HAMELIN JOANNE HAMELIN JOSEPH
PETER HAMELIN JUDY HAMELIN BARBARA A HAMILTON BRIAN HAMILTON GORDON HAMILTON JAMES S. HAMILTON STANLEY T HAMILTON MICHAEL T HAMMOND RICHARD
HAMMOND TONY HAMMOND TONY HAMMOND CATHERINE HAMPTON AHMED HANAFI DENNIS HANCOCK DEREK HANCOCK EDGAR HANCOCK GORDON S. HANCOCK KENNETH
HANCOCK ROSEMARY HANCOCK CHARLES W HAND PIERCE M HAND GERALD HANDFORD TIMOTHY HANEL CHUI HANG FUI HANG DALE HANNIGAN MICHAEL HANNIGAN EUGENE
P HANNON LEONARD HANSEN PETER HANSEN RAYMOND HANSEN VALARIE HANSEN DELORES HANSON GRAHAM HANSON JO A HANSON PARMINDER HANSRA RAZAUL HAQUE
DAVID HARDING DONALD HARDING PAMELA HARDING ROBERT W. HARDING STANLEY G HARDING THOMAS D. HARDING WANDA HARDING PATRICK HARDMAN DARREN K HARDY
JAMES A R HARGREAVES BRENT HARLE DAVID C HARLEY JR DAVID HARLEY SR. MARJORIE HARMSEN AARON HARNETT CAROL HARNETT DAVID HARNETT PLEMAN HARNETT
RAYMOND HARNETT ALBERT HARPE E KEVIN HARPE FRED HARPE HENRY HARPE ROLAND HARPE DARYL HARPER CAROL HARQUAIL CHRISTOPHER W. HARRIS DAVID L. HARRIS
LEONARD G. HARRIS MARGARET HARRIS RANDY HARRIS RON G HARRIS BRUCE HARRISON DANA HARRISON JOHN W. HARRISON PHILIP J HARRISON RUBY HARRISON STEPHEN
HARRISON BERTHA HART BRUCE A HART DEREK G HART GLORIA A. HART KEVIN J. HART JAMES A. HARTE ROBERT HARTLEY LYONEL E HARTMAN DAVID B. HARVEY KELLY HASLETT
DEBRA HATCH DWAYNE HATCH EAON R. HATCH KIM HATCH BRIAN HATFIELD DENNIS HAW ALLAN G. HAWCO PATRICK HAWCO PATRICK HAWKINS JAMES M HAY BRIAN J. HAYES
GEORGE HAYES ISABEL HAYES KEN L. HAYWARD LEITA HAYWARD STANLEY HAYWARD MIKE E. HAZELWOOD JOHN R. HEAD RONALD HEADGE GERALD F.S. HEADON VICTORIA
S R HEADON MICHAEL HEALY RONALD H HEAP MIKE HEARN JUANITA HEATH OLIVER HEATH PATRICK HEATH AUDREY J HEATHERINGTON DOUGLAS HEATON ROGER
HEBBLETHWAITE SHAWN M. HEBBLETHWAITE GEORGE HEBERT LYLE HECK NANCY HECKER PHILIP HEDDERLY GLEN HEDLEY HANS H. HEGGEN BRIAN HEIBERT NORMAN W. HEIN
HANS A HEINEMANN BERNICE HEINZ ROBERT HEINZ PAUL HEISING GILBERT S HELLIER JOHN HELM MICHAEL HELM CHRISTINE HELMAN FREDERICK A. HEMPHILL SANDRA
HEMPHILL BRADLEY HEMSTOCK HENRY J. HENDER DALE HENDERSON LINELLE HENDERSON ANITA HENDRICKS ELAINE HENNIG GARRY D HENNINGS LAWRENCE E. HENRY LOUIS
HENSEL TREVOR HENSMAN PETER HERBERT SANDRA HERBERT TREVOR HERLE NEIL HERRICK PAUL HETHERINGTON LAWRENCE HEW STEPHEN HEW ELIZABETH HEWSON
MICHAEL HEWSON DAVID HEYSER LAWRENCE A. HIBBARD GLENN W HICKE ANDRE HICKEY CONNIE G.M. HICKEY KENDALL C HICKEY ROBERT HICKEY MICKEY L. HICKS DOUGLAS
HICOX DONALD HIGDON JOHN HIGDON MARK HIGHFIELD BRUCE HILDRED WAYNE D HILDRED DONALD HILL JOHNATHAN R. HILL KEITH MARTIN HILL PEARL HILL WM. JOHN HILL
GLEN ALLEN HILLCOX ALLAN HILLIER RAYMOND HILLIER JIM L. HILSENTEGER ERIC HINCHCLIFFE SCOTT WALTER HINDLE DWIGHT HINES LINDSAY HINES DOUG HINGLEY LOUIS
S. HINKO ARTHUR A. HINTZ ANDERSON J. HIPSON CALVIN HISCOCK DONALD HISCOCK GORDON HISCOCK HAROLD F HISCOX DAVID A.S. HISEY CALVIN HOBBS ELIZABETH HOBBS
JOSEPH HOBBS RESHELDA HOBBS CATHY HOCHHAUSEN DANIEL F. HOCHHAUSEN BRIAN HOCKER CHERYL HOCKER MIKE HOCKER LEANDER HODDER LEONARD HODDER SAM H
HODDER BONNIE L. HODDINOTT JEFFREY HODDINOTT NOLAN HODDINOTT GERALD HODGE JOHN HODGE DOUGLAS HODGINS LEE A HODGINS MARK HODGINS NEIL HODGINS
JIM HODGKINSON BAYNE HODGSON CAM HODGSON CURTIS HODGSON DELBERT P HODGSON DWILA HODGSON MARK HODGSON WENDELL D HODGSON RANDY A. HOEHNE
EVA HOFBAUER KARL HOFBAUER WILBERT J. HOFLIN DOUGLAS HOGAN JOSEPH G. HOGAN MICHAEL G HOGAN LYLE HOGARTH DON HOGGARTH TERRYANN HOGGARTH WAYNE
HOGGARTH JOHN HOLDEN FREDERICK E HOLESWORTH DENISE HOLLETT ALLAN W. HOLLOWAY LYNDA HOLLOWAY MELVIN HOLLOWAY ROY HOLLOWAY TERRANCE HOLLOWAY
WILLIAM J. H. HOLLOWAY WILLIAM T HOLLOWAY DARREN HOLMES GEORGE HOLMES HAZEN J. HOLMES STEVEN HOLMES DONALD HOLT JOHN H. HOLT KIM HOLTZHAUER RAY
HOLTZHAUER TRUDY HOLTZHAUER MICHAEL R HOLUK NYUK-HIN HON DANNY HOOD RANDALL HOOD IAN HOPE JOHN HOPKINS MICHAEL HOPKINS TENLEY HOPKINS WILLIAM
HOPKINS ROLF HOPKINSON DEAN M HOPPING BRUCE HORE DONALD C. HORRICK STEVEN DOUGLAS HORSLEY ROBERT WILLIAM HORSMAN CONRAD HORVATH JEROME HOSKINS
LEO HOSKINS CHESTER G HOUG KEVIN HOUG MAUREEN HOUGHTON ROBERT E. HOUGHTON DOMINIC HOUSE LEVON G. HOVAGIMIAN AUSTIN T.J. HOWARD DIANA HOWARD JANE
HOWARD KERRIE-ANN HOWARD KEVIN HOWARD MARIE HOWARD WALLACE HOWARD ROBERT HOWATT J. F. BRIAN HOWE PETER WESLEY HOWE ADLOR HOWELL GRANT HOWELL
JAMES HOWELL ROBERT J. HOWELL DARREN HOWSE JOHN HOWSE MIKE HOWSE PIUS HOWSE TROY HOWSE R.E. HOYLE BAXTER S. HOYLES PAUL P. HRABEC LUBOMIR HRAZDIRA
ROBERT HRYCIUK CHONG HSUNG DEREK HUBAND PETER HUBBARD WILLIAM HUBBARD BEATRICE L. HUDDLESTON JIRI HUDECEK ROBERT HUDSON WILLIAM B HUDSON STEVEN
EDWARD HUDY OSWALD HUEBNER ROSS HUEBNER BERNARD HUGHES JOHN HUGHES TREVOR LA HUGHES DARREL HULAN HAZEL HULAN JOANNE HULAN MICHAEL J. HULAN
GORDON HULL BRAD HUMBLE DARRELL HUMPHREY FLOYD HUMPHREY TIMOTHY HUMPHREY CECIL J. HUNT GENE HUNT JOHN HUNT LORNE HUNT LOYAL M. HUNT RONALD S
HUNT TAMRA HUNT THOMAS R HUNT TRUMAN HUNT D BLAIR HUNTER HUGH W HUNTER JEFFREY HUNTER JERRY HUNTER RONALD HUNTER LLOYD HUPPIE LYLE HUPPIE PAT
HUPPIE WAYNE D HUPPIE SAJEED HUQ D. REGINALD HURFORD LOWEN HURFORD MICHAEL HURLBURT PATRICK P J HURLEY RAYMOND HURLEY STEPHEN HURLEY THOMAS J.P.
HURLEY TOM HURST GILBERT G. HURTUBISE RAMONA HURTUBISE MOHAMED HUSAIN ZORIDA HUSAIN WALLY HUSKA JAMES HUSSEY YVONNE HUSSYNEC TONY C HUTCHINGS
G V HUTCHINSON JOHN HUTCHISON KEITH HUTCHISON SCOTT HUTTON DON HUTZKAL SHIRLEE HUTZKAL ROGER HUXTER PATRICK HUYBRECHT GORDON HYATT ROBERT HYATT
A. W. HYNDMAN CAROLINE HYNDMAN ANDREW J. HYNES EDGAR HYNES HANK HYNES JERRY HYNES JOSEPH F. HYNES MELITA HYNES PAULINE HYSKA BRUCE INGLIS NORMAN
INGRAM NORMAN F. INKSTER LEON IRLA VERLEEN IRONSIDE GRANT IRWIN PATRICK IRWIN THOMAS IRWIN BYRON A ISAAC GRISELDA ISAAC ROOSEVELT A. ISAAC DAVID ISAAK
WALLY IWANKOW DOUGLAS IWASKOW LAURA-LEE IWASKOW NORMAN P IWASKOW ADRIENNE JACK LESTER J JACKMAN DAVID JACKSON STANLEY JACKSON HUBERT JACOBS
MAYNARD H. JACOBS ROSALIND JACOBS FITZGERALD JAGBANDHANSINGH SHARLEEN D. JAGER EDWARD JAHELKA ROY JAHELKA THOMAS JAHELKA FIROZ A JAKHURA
DOUGLAS JAMES ERROL JAMES GEORGE JAMES GLENN JAMES LEANNE JAMES WAYNE JAMEUS ANN JAMIESON DONNA JAMIESON MARK E JAMIESON ROY JAMIESON
CATHERINE JANES ERIC JANES LEONARD H JANES KENNETH JANKE JOSEPH JANKOWSKI BRIAN JANSEN GERARD JANSEN WAYNE JANSEN ANGELO JANVIER DOREEN JANVIER
GORDON S JANVIER JOANNE JANVIER MARCEL THOMAS JANVIER RAYMOND JANVIER RONALD JANVIER JACK JANZEN DWIGHT JANZER ERWIN F. JARDINE SHAWN JARDINE
SUZANNE JARDINE GAMELA JARKAS GARY JARL IGNATIUS ROBERT JARVIS ROBERT JARVIS STEPHEN JARVIS NORMAN JASTER ANTONI JASTRZEBSKI ROBERT JASTRZEBSKI
ALFRED JAYE MICHEL JEAN DARRELL E. JEFFREY COLIN J. JEGOU NORMAN ROBERT JELFS JOHN A. JELLY ALAN J JENKINS DENISE M JENNER DENYS JENNER JAMES JENNER
LOREEN JENNER DOUGLAS JENSEN SUSAN JENSEN B JERCHEL CALINA JERCHEL PETER JERCHEL KAREN JESSO PATRICK JESSO WAYNE F. JESSOME NIZAR A. JETHA ROLAND
JETTE ERNEST JICKELS RODNEY JIMMO RUSTAM T. JIWAN JOHN MORLEY JODREY GARETH ES JOHN DAVID R JOHNSON GEORGE JOHNSON GREG JOHNSON HAROLD V. A.
JOHNSON LARRY JOHNSON PAUL JOHNSON PAUL A.K. JOHNSON S. CHARLENE JOHNSON STEWART JOHNSON THOMAS JOHNSON THOMAS C JOHNSON WAYNE JOHNSON WES
JOHNSON GREGORY JOHNSTON HARVEY W. JOHNSTON KEN JONAH CLIFFORD JONASSON JOHN JONASSON LORRAINE JONASSON VALERIE JONASSON ALUN JONES BARRIE
JONES DAVID JONES GARRY L. JONES GEORGE JONES GWENFFRA JONES JOHN J. JONES KAREN JONES PHILIP JONES ROLAND JONES SHEILA JONES JACK JORGENSEN ELSIE
JOSEPH GEORGE JOSEPH CHRISTOPHER JOYCE DONNA L. JOYCE GARY JOYCE JOE JOYCE KATHLEEN JOYCE FRANK L. JUDGE MICHAEL S. JUKOSKY CHRIS JURY NICK KACSMARIK
SUSAN KACSMARIK KENNETH J. KADOSKI MARK KADY AZAMUL KAHRIM EDWARD C KAINE FRANK KALHS DEBI L KALININ ROGER KALININ JOHN PAUL KALNINS JANET KALYN
WAYNE KALYNUIK KARIM S. KAMIL BRENT A. KAMINSKI VIC P. KAMINSKY GREY J. KAMPALA TERRY KANE VICTOR KAPANEN EDMUND F. KAPAU-AN ASHOK K. KAPOOR DOUGLAS
KARMEN ROLF KARMSTEN MAEVE KAVANAGH NOEL A. KAVANAGH TIMOTHY J. KAY VICTOR KAYS MICHAEL G. KAZAMEL EDWARD KAZMIERCZAK PAUL KEARNEY RAYMOND D.
KEATING KEVIN KEATS PERRY R. KEATS GARY KEAYS DONALD KEENAN KENNETH KEENAN CHARLES KEENE WILLIAM KEENE BERNADETTE KEEPING AUDREY J. KEHLERT LEO KEITH
LEONARD KELLER MURRAY KELLINGTON BRIAN D. KELLY DAVID J. KELLY EDWARD KELLY JOYCE KELLY MARILYN KELLY MILES KELLY MITCHELL KELLY WILLIAM KELLY JANET
E KELSEY BARBARA KENDALL DAVID B KENDALL HARRY T KENDALL ROY KENDELL EDWARD P KENNEALY ROBERT D KENNEALY BETTY KENNEDY DARLENE KENNEDY DONALD
KENNEDY R. DOUGLAS KENNETT WILLIAM KENNEY COLIN G KERR GERARD KERRIGAN PHILIP KERSEY DERRICK KERSHAW AFZAL KHAN EDWARD H. KHAN TUPHAIL M KHAN PHIL
KICKSEE GEORGE THOMSON KIDD HAROLD KIDD RONALD KIDD SUSAN KIDD JOHN P. KILBOY KENNETH R KILBURN GERALD F. KILPATRICK WILLIAM KILPATRICK JOHN KILSDONK
MARTIN JOHN KILSDONK JOEL KIMBALL THEODORE KINASH BERNARD KING BRUCE KING DENNIS W KING FRAN KING GWENDOLYN P KING LLOYD W KING MONROE KING RANDY
KING RICHARD D. KING ROBERT W. KING ROGER KING ROGER J KING ROGER N. KING SCOTT KING THADDEUS KING WESLEY KING GERRY W. KINGDON CHARLES KINGSTON
CATHERINE KINNELL DAVID KINNEY MADONNA KIRBY ROGER P KIRCHEN DR MICHELE KIRICHENKO ROBERT KIRICHENKO BELA KISH RICK KISH TIMOTHY KITCHEN TED KIZIOR ROY
KJELSHUS RUDY H. KLAUS HORST A. KLAWIKOWSKI DENNIS KLEIN ROGER KLEINSCHROTH RAYMOND KLEM SHAWN KLIMCHUK MIKE M KLIMEK EDUARD L KLINK LOGEMAN
MICHAEL R KLIPPENSTEIN BEVERLY KNIBB SANDRA KNIBB JOYCE KNIGHT SHIRLEY KNIGHT ANNA KNISTER DARRELL KNISTER KELLY KNISTER KEVIN KNOWLES MICHAEL
KNOWLES DONALD KNOX EDWARD KNOX RHONDA KNUTSON MIROSLAV KOCMAN GLEN KOHLSMITH JOSHUA M. KOKARAM PETER S KOKARAM JOHN KOKIW ALOIS KOLINSKY
KATHRYN P KOLLROSS JANICE KOLOMYJEC LORINDA KONG NELSON KONG STEVE KONG PETER KONING BOHDAN KONOWALEC STEVE KONOWALEC OWEN KONSKI RHONDA
KOOISTRA TONY R KOOPMANS CAMILLE KOOTENAY PATRICIA KOOTENAY DEBORAH M KOSHER ANDY KOSTIUK JAMES KOSTIUK NICK KOSTIUK ARIE E KOUDYS ELISABETH
KOUDYS ERNIE KOWALSKI LORNA J. KOWALSKI HUGH KOYATA MARLENE KOZAK EVELYN KOZIOL WILLIAM D. KOZLUK GERRY KRAUSE LINDSAY KRAUSERT RONALD KREUTZER
FRED KRIEGER ARNOLD KRIEWALDT NORM KRISTJANSSON AUDREY H. KRUEGER HEATHER J KRUEGER VERLAYNE KRYSAK LECH KRZYWOBLOCKI LEO KUCY LORNA KUCY ERWIN
KUHR JOSEF KULDASEK KRIS KUMAR SATISH KUMAR SAMUEL KUMSON PATRICK J KUPROWSKI EDWARD KUS SYLVER P. KUSHNIRUK KARLA KUTTMANN WILLIAM KUTTMANN
GEOFF KUTZ PAUL KUZMA WAI-LAU KWOK TEDDY KWONG MURRAY L'HEUREUX PAUL A. L'HEUREUX RAYMOND R. LABELLE CONSTANCE LABERGE MICHEL LABERGE GEORGE
W. LABINE J. LABONTE PHILIP C. LACHAMBRE HECTOR LACHANCE ROLAND LACHANCE ROBERT LACOMBE ANDRE LACOSTE NORMAN LACOURCIERE FRANK W. LACROIX BRIAN
A LADE EDMOND LADOUCEUR LINDA LADOUCEUR PETER A. LADOUCEUR RENE LADOUCEUR RONALD A LADOUCEUR ANNILA LAEEQUE ISHRAT LAEEQUE JOSEPH LAFOND
LEONARD LAFOND RICHARD D LAHAIE JOSEPH V. LAHEY LARRY LALONDE RICHARD G. LALONDE WILLIAM ARNOLD LALONDE MICHAEL LAM WILLIAM LAM DAVID LAMB STEPHEN
C. LAMB BRIAN LAMOND PATRICK L LAMPING DAVID R. LANDGRAFF NEIL LANDRY PETER LANDRY JACK LANE JAMES R LANE RENATA LANGAN JOHN LANGERAK AUREL U.
LANGEVIN GUY LANGILLE MIKE J LANGLOIS PIERRE LANGLOIS LYLE LANGMAID JACQUES LANOUE EMILE LAPOINTE LYNN LARDEN ADRIAN LARKIN EDGAR LAROCQUE PATRICK
LAROUE EDWARD LARSEN GORDON RONALD LARSON JOE LARSON GORDON LASAGA ROBERT LASALLE OTTO LASKA ELOISA B LAU SHEK NGAR LAU MALCOLM LAURIE PAUL
C LAVENDER RICHARD LAVENTURE PAUL LAVERDIERE VERONICA LAVERS MABEL LAVIOLETTE DOUGLAS E. LAVOIE GEOFFREY D. LAW LLOYD LAWLEY GARY LAWRENCE ROBERT
JAMES LAWRENCE SAM LAWRENCE CAROLLE LAWRIE JOYCE M LAWRIE PETER LAWRIE RICHARD LAY HEATHER (BONNIE) LAYBOURNE BENEDICT LAYS ANDREA LE CLAIR
BERNARD LE CLAIR ADOLPH LE ROUX DENIS R. LEADBEATER MICHAEL LEAHY CLIFFORD W LEAR LINDA LEAVEY LOUIS LEAVEY MICHEL LEAVEY DAVID LEBEDYNSKI EMILE
LEBEDYNSKI GINO LEBEUF EUDORE G LEBLANC FRANK LEBLANC GERARD G. LEBLANC GORDON L LEBLANC JACK A. LEBLANC JOHN LEBLANC LAWRENCE LEBLANC RICHARD
LEBLANC GERALD F. LEBRETON WAYNE LEBRUN CATHERYN LECK RONALD LECK ROBERT THOMAS LECLAIR TRUDY LEDDY BARRY LEDREW LEIGHTON LEDREW CLEVE J. LEE CHEE
PATRICIA LEE CHEE ANDREW LEE ANDY LEE DAVID LEE GEOFFREY LEE GORDON C. LEE GORDON R LEE JENNIFER LEE JOHN LEE JUNG J. LEE KHAI-TIONG LEE LESLIE LEE MARJORIE
LEE STEPHEN LEE STEPHEN LEE DOMINIC LEFRESNE MARCELLE LEFRESNE COLLEEN LEGDON ED M. LEHBAUER DONALD LEHMANN KENNETH C. LEIBEL INEZ LEIGH SHARON

THE
SYNCRUDE
STORY

THE
SYNCRUDE
STORY

In Our Own Words

Syncrude Canada Ltd.

Copyright © Syncrude Canada Ltd., December 1990
P.O. Bag 4023, M.D. 1000, Fort McMurray, Alberta T9H 3H5

First Edition, December 1990

Published by Syncrude Canada Ltd.,
Communications Division, Human Resources.
For more information, call (403) 790-6403

Editor: Barbara Bellemare
Writers: Lois Bridges, Marg Pullishy, Jody MacPherson
Editorial Assistant/Photo Editor: John Cooper
Marketing: Nancy Grenier
Design and Production: Cheryl Lieberman and John Luckhurst/GDL
Cover Design: Cheryl Lieberman
Colour Separations: The Graphic Edge
Printing: Quality Colour

Acknowledgements: Phil Lachambre, Luba Cymbalisty,
Don Thompson, Vic Kaminsky, Mavis Walmsley

This book is dedicated
to the vision of Frank Spragins
and the employees, owners
contractors and suppliers
who helped him achieve it.

Contents

1 THE EARLY YEARS *3*

2 IT'S A GO! *25*

3 CONSTRUCTION FEVER *39*

4 THERE'S NO PLACE LIKE IT *55*

5 START UP *71*

6 GROWING PAINS *87*

7 THE WAY AHEAD *103*

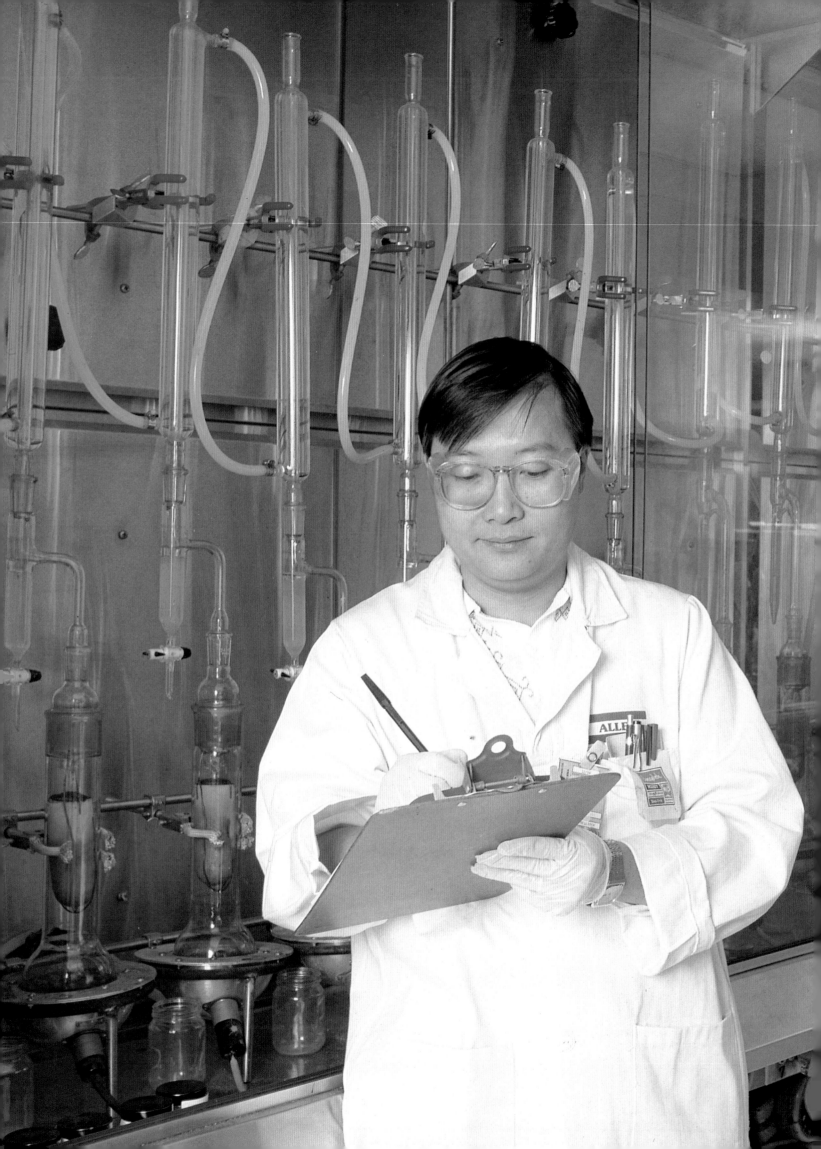

The Northern Alberta Railway, from its earliest days, had an important role in the development of the oil sands.

In the late 1940s, Fort McMurray, in northeastern Alberta, was little more than a collection of rustic wooden buildings nestled in a misty hidden valley in the middle of a vast wilderness.

Home to hundreds of natives indigenous to the area, plus a handful of trappers, miners and adventurers, the region was at the beginning of a great frontier.

The area's harsh, often bitter winter weather was only for those too frost-seasoned to be intimidated by the elements. Spring in the North brought some relief — as well as puddles of mud that made mothers shudder and children laugh with delight. Summers also presented a challenge, punctuated by a tangle of

Dr. Karl A. Clark working on the early extraction process, in his lab at the University of Alberta, in the 1920s.

blistering hot days and the occasional buzz of marauding insect troops.

Snuggled in at the junction of the Clearwater, Athabasca, Horse and Hangingstone Rivers, only a few men and women could have seen the potential for such an alien land.

But they weren't alone. The Alberta government, anxious to access the oil of the northeast quadrant of the province, bought the 500 ton oil sands separation plant at Bitumount in 1948.

Interest in oil sands technology was growing rapidly, attracting some of the brightest, most progressive minds in the world. Their mission was to extract rich, abundant oil from muskeg, rock, sand and clay. Some

---

Left: The early years: Franklin Avenue, Fort McMurray.

Right: A bucket, pulled by a winch and guided by a man, was the original dragline used to mine oil sand.

favored a hot water extraction process; others opted for the "in situ" method which uses heat to separate oil from sand still locked in the ground.

And so began a mission that would change the face of the province and ultimately impact on the world oil market.

Day by day, year by year, young men and women made their way to Oil Sands Country. It offered them unprecedented challenges and the opportunity to be leaders in industrial development. The downside was the isolation and lack of basic comforts; amenities which were increasingly expected and savored in the post-war years.

Their journey would be checkered by extraordinary disappointments and even more extraordinary victories. It would span several decades; involve more than one provincial premier; and, ultimately require the talents of a multitude of people undaunted by the narrow boundaries of time, space and technology.

They were pioneers in their own right, instinctively knowing they were creating history. Their work and commitment would forever change the oil industry in Alberta, as they slowly unlocked the secret of spinning liquid gold from the oil sands.

I nterest in Alberta's oil sands extended far beyond the province's boundaries. For years, Cities Service Company, based in Lake Charles, Louisiana, had workers ship buckets of oil sands to their refinery so they could test the warm water extraction process. Encouraged by the results, the company bought controlling interest in the Bitumount plant in 1958. It subsequently built "a small by today's standards", 35 tons per hour pilot plant at Mildred Lake.

By then, power brokers in the oil industry were eyeing Alberta's north — some with skepticism, some with guarded optimism, most with enthusiasm. Recognizing a need for a cohesive, coordinated approach in

developing the area, the primary players in the oil sands game combined their financial and human resources. Royalite Oil Company Limited combined with Gulf Oil. Cities Service Research and Development Co. was joined by Imperial Oil Limited and Atlantic Richfield Canada Ltd.

Glacial Drift
Shale
Sand
Bituminous Sands
Limestone
Salt
Dolomite
Granite

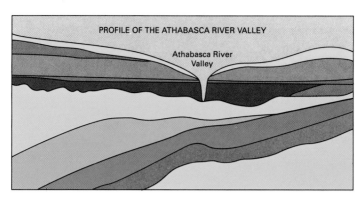

PROFILE OF THE ATHABASCA RIVER VALLEY

Athabasca River Valley

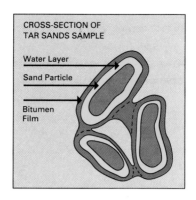

CROSS-SECTION OF TAR SANDS SAMPLE

Water Layer
Sand Particle
Bitumen Film

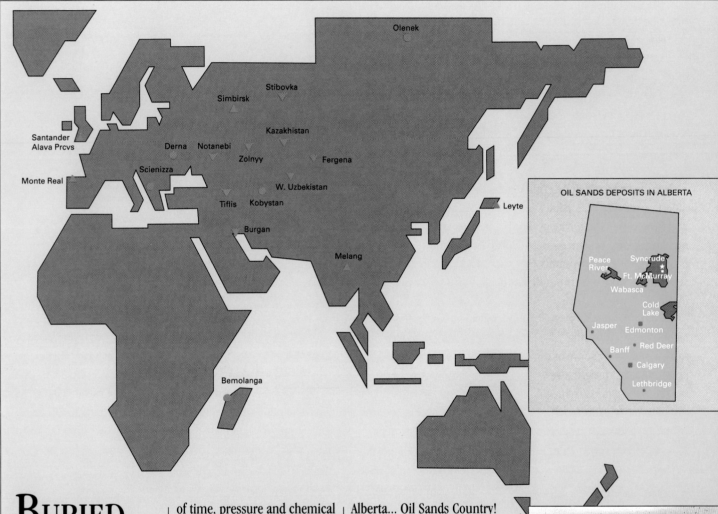

Olenek

Stibovka

Simbirsk

Santander Alava Prcvs

Kazakhistan

Derna   Notanebi

Zolnyy   Fergena

Scienizza

Monte Real

W. Uzbekistan

Tiflis   Kobystan

Burgan

Leyte

Melang

Bemolanga

OIL SANDS DEPOSITS IN ALBERTA

Peace River   Syncrude
Ft. McMurray
Wabasca
Cold Lake
Jasper   Edmonton
Banff   Red Deer
Calgary
Lethbridge

BURIED TREASURE

HUNDREDS OF millions of years ago, seas covered the vast majority of the earth. The water was a haven and home for an endless array of tiny creatures and vegetation. With the passage of time, pressure and chemical action, underwater life took on a new form in death... and became oil.

Over millions of years, layers of rock built up at the bottom of the seas. Volcanoes and earthquakes changed the surface of the earth, causing the land and water to shift, settle and eventually seep into the surface of the region we now know as northern Alberta... Oil Sands Country!

Nature gave Canadians a treasure of oil trapped in time; a bounty so rich it is estimated to be five times larger than the Saudi Arabian reserves!

Layers of oil sand are clearly seen in this photo of the box cut in the mine.

Before the days of pipelines, the International Bitumen Co. transported its bitumen in barrels.

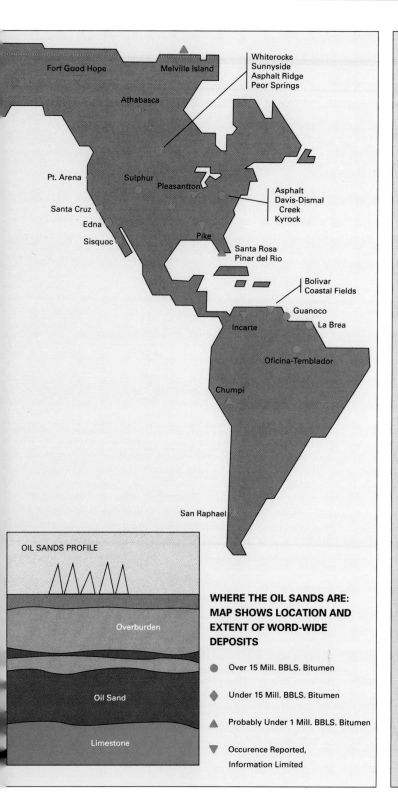

OIL SANDS PROFILE

Overburden

Oil Sand

Limestone

WHERE THE OIL SANDS ARE: MAP SHOWS LOCATION AND EXTENT OF WORD-WIDE DEPOSITS

● Over 15 Mill. BBLS. Bitumen

◆ Under 15 Mill. BBLS. Bitumen

▲ Probably Under 1 Mill. BBLS. Bitumen

▽ Occurence Reported, Information Limited

WEATHER WOES: TOO MUCH OF A GOOD THING

IN THE EARLY 1950S, NOT EVERYONE was inspired by the pioneering spirit or overly impressed with Alberta's Oil Sand Country.

After visiting the site, a young reporter from the "Oil and Gas Journal", clearly bridled his enthusiasm for the area's natural environment, which he judiciously described as "inhospitable". He wrote: "From the time the snow flies in September or October, winter grips the isolated camp until April. The mercury plunges as low as 59 degrees below zero. When the thaw finally comes, much of the country is bottomless muskeg that can swallow a man or drilling rig. The searing heat of summer sometimes sends the thermometer to 105 degrees."

During the cold winter months, dog sleds were used for transportation from Lower Camp to Fort McMurray.

IT CAME OUT IN THE WASH

MRS. GORDON COULSON must have been a pillar of strength, humor and tenderness, living as she did with a man determined to separate sand and clay from the precious oil rooted deeply in Alberta's oil sands. But it's hard to imagine what her husband said when she demanded:

"Gordon, what have you done to my washing machine?"

What first appeared to be a man doing his fair share of the household chores, in the early 1950s, quickly proved incorrect. The innovative Mr. Coulson had instead dumped a gooey mixture of water, kerosene, sand and clay where there should have been laundry and detergent. The Calgary contractor, inspired by the gyrations of the machine, was convinced that spinning the mixture long and hard enough would sift out the waste material and retain the oil.

He wasn't far off.

As founder of Can-Amera

Aerial view of Fort McMurray in the late 1940s.

Above: Lower Camp looking out over Horseshoe Lake. Circa 1963.

Left: Draper's experimental oil sands plant in Waterways.

"WHEN I WAS GROWING UP IN FORT MCMURRAY, I HEARD A LOT ABOUT THE OIL SANDS, BUT IT DIDN'T MEAN MUCH TO ME. WE HAD A HUGE SWIMMING HOLE NEAR THE OLD ABASANDS SITE, AND IN THE SUMMER WE'D SPEND HOURS THERE. AFTER OUR SWIM, WE WOULD WANDER AROUND IN OUR BARE FEET, EXPLORING LIKE ALL KIDS DO, AND BECAUSE THERE WAS SO MUCH TAR IN THE SOIL, WE'D GO HOME JUST COATED IN THE STUFF. EVERYDAY, OUR MOTHER WOULD GIVE US HELL, DRAG OUT THE CLEANING FLUID AND MAKE US WASH THE TAR OFF OUR FEET... SO UNTIL I WAS AN ADULT, I ALWAYS ASSOCIATED THE OIL SANDS WITH CHAFFED FEET!"

BRIAN CLARK, ARTIST, FORMER FORT MCMURRAY RESIDENT

The Abasand plant in the early 1940s.

Large photo and inset: Bitumount, a provincial historic resource, is located 89 kilometres north of Fort McMurray. It ceased operations in 1958.

Export and Refining Company Limited, Coulson, struck a deal with Royalite that would take his research out of the kitchen and into the laboratory so he could further develop and explore his centrifugal separation process.

He paid $180,000 for the Bitumount plant in 1955 and considerably less for his wife's new washing machine.

"IN THOSE EARLY DAYS, EVERY TIME YOU TURNED A CORNER
YOU CAME UP AGAINST ANOTHER CHALLENGE, AND SOMETIMES
YOU FELT IT MIGHT BE INSURMOUNTABLE. BUT WE HAD A
BRILLIANT 'BRAIN POOL' PEOPLE , LIKE CONSULTANT LINCOLN
CLARK WHO WERE DRIVEN BY DREAMS, NOT DOLLARS. FRANK
SPRAGINS ENCOURAGED US AND URGED US TO OVERCOME THE
PROBLEMS...IT WAS THE MEN AGAINST THE MACHINES; NOW I KNOW
THE MEN WON."

LUBA CYMBALISTY, RESEARCH

Despite a shaky start, riddled with ups and downs, delays and a lack of funding, a major research and testing program was eventually set up in 1960 and conducted at the Mildred Lake project site next to where Suncor now sits on the shores of the Athabasca. Though remote and rustic by today's standards, the project included: a large extraction

The first bucketwheel in North America was used to mine the oil sand at Lower Camp. Circa 1960.

facility, steam and power plants, shops, a laboratory, warehouses, an air strip, housing and a commissary for a crew that numbered about 125.

Mining and materials handling equipment drifted up the river by barge, or was airlifted in on a DC 3 that brought men, machines and materials to the site at least twice each day. When all else failed, developers followed the path of the fur traders bringing the gear up by a combination of land and water routes.

With little understanding of the whims of nature, the enormity of the task at hand, or the government's concern about venturing into speculative enterprises, the long and arduous labor that would eventually result in the emergence of Syncrude began.

Above: Life in the camp in 1960 was not all work. There was also lots of camaraderie and recreation.

Panabodes were the original research camp housing units. They were used during the early 1960s.

Today's giant bucketwheels are used to mine the oil sand. A bucketwheel is almost twice the size of a football field and measures 140 metres in length.

In 1958, Cities Service announced plans to go ahead with the "...most comprehensive research project ever undertaken to release liquid hydrocarbons from the Athabasca oil sands of northern Alberta..." While developments were on-going at Syncrude, Great Canadian Oil Sands Limited (GCOS), now known as Suncor, applied to the Alberta Oil and Gas Conservation Board, forerunner of the present-day Energy Resources Conservation Board, for a permit to build a 31,500 barrel a day plant.

The early sixties were important years for the oil sands. New technologies were emerging to accommodate the special needs created by large volumes of production and often frigid weather patterns. No doubt, positive test results were a major factor in helping reinforce the viability of developing the oil sands.

Cities Service was confident the time was ripe to proceed with a commercial oil sands plant. On May 9, 1962, the company applied for a license to produce 100,000 barrels of synthetic crude oil daily. While the Alberta Oil and Gas Conservation Board mulled

The original bucketwheel used at Lower Camp is now located at Heritage Park in Fort McMurray.

THERE'S NO PLACE LIKE... LOWER CAMP

THE MILDRED LAKE pilot plant, on the banks of the Athabasca River, seemed quite remote from the sleek metropolitan offices of its four powerful oil company owners or even the company's Edmonton office which was made up of about 50 engineering and office staff. The original pilot plant later became known as Lower Camp, a large housing complex for workers.

"THE FIRST TIME I EVER CAME TO THE SITE, I WAS A 23 YEAR OLD KID. I FLEW INTO MCMURRAY, SAW THREE FIGHTS, SPENT A SLEEPLESS NIGHT IN THE HOTEL, AND THEN CAME TO THE SITE THE NEXT MORNING BY BOAT. I'D NEVER SEEN ANYTHING LIKE IT. THERE IT WAS, SITTING IN THE MIDDLE OF NOWHERE. THE PILOT SITE WAS ALREADY OPERATIONAL...WE WORKED HARD. AT THE END OF THE DAY, WE CAME BACK TO QUARTERS THAT WERE VERY COMFORTABLE, IF NOT OPULENT, AND ATE SOME OF THE BEST MEALS I'VE EVER EATEN!"

TOM WILD, ENGINEERING

"ONE NIGHT THINGS GOT A LITTLE OUT OF HAND...ONE OF THE GUYS, WHOSE NAME I WON'T MENTION, HAD BEEN 'ELBOW BENDING' PRETTY HARD AND FINALLY JUST PASSED OUT. A FEW OF US SLIPPED INTO MEDICAL SERVICES AND "BORROWED" THE STUFF WE NEEDED TO PUT HIM IN A CAST FROM HIP TO TOE. WE DID A PRETTY GOOD JOB; HE DIDN'T SUSPECT A THING WHEN HE WOKE UP THE NEXT MORNING. WE TOLD HIM HE'D TAKEN A BAD FALL AND HAD TO STAY IN THE CAST FOR AT LEAST SIX WEEKS. AFTER ABOUT THREE DAYS OF WATCHING HIM HOBBLE AROUND THE CAMP, SOMEONE FINALLY TOLD HIM THE TRUTH!"

WILBUR GRAHAM,
RETIRED, SYNCRUDE MINING

"THERE WAS A REALLY STRONG SENSE OF COMMUNITY AT LOWER CAMP. WE WORKED TOGETHER, PLAYED TOGETHER AND LIVED TOGETHER. I REMEMBER ONE TIME, WE WANTED TO BUILD A CURLING RINK. WE GOT A LITTLE LUMBER AND A LOT OF THE GUYS, AND SPENT A WEEKEND BUILDING IT. IT HAD ONLY A COUPLE OF SHEETS OF ICE, BUT LET ME TELL YOU, WITH EVERYBODY WORKING DIFFERENT SHIFTS, THAT RINK WAS BUSY ALMOST 24 HOURS A DAY, EVERY DAY!"

WALTER RILKOFF, RETIRED
EMPLOYEE, CITIES SERVICE
AND SYNCRUDE

"THOSE EARLY YEARS WERE RE-MARKABLE. THERE WERE A HAND-FUL OF MEN...DEDICATED, STRONG-WILLED AND ABLE TO CONVINCE OTHERS OF THE VIA-BILITY OF THE PROJECT. THEY WERE MORE COMMITTED TO IT THAN THE STATE OF TECHNOL-OGY WARRANTED...BUT THEY WERE MEN OF VISION...MEN WHO WERE DETERMINED TO DO WHAT IT TOOK TO TURN A DREAM INTO A REALITY."

RON GRAY, EARLY RESEARCH
EMPLOYEE AND RETIRED MANAGER,
MILDRED LAKE PILOT PLANT

"WORKING CONDITIONS AT THE MILDRED LAKE PILOT PLANT COULD BE PRETTY MISERABLE, ESPECIALLY WHEN THE UNIT PLUGGED UP AND YOU WERE UP TO YOUR KNEES IN MUCK. STILL, IT WAS GOOD TRAINING. IT MADE YOU APPRECIATE THE FINER THINGS IN LIFE—LIKE NOT BEING SOAKED IN SOLVENT, HAVING SAND IN YOUR BOOTS, OR BEING COVERED WITH TAR."

GEORGE WILLIAMSON,
RETIRED EMPLOYEE,
CITIES SERVICE AND
SYNCRUDE

"WE WERE ALL KIDS AT THE TIME AND WILLING TO LIVE BY THE RULES...OR AT LEAST MOST OF THE RULES...LIKE NO WOMEN OR ALCOHOL IN CAMP, HONORING MEAL TIMES, AND MAKING OUR OWN BEDS. NOW, I DON'T REMEM-BER ANYONE EVER SNEAKING A WOMAN IN FOR THE EVENING, BUT I DO REMEMBER A FEW QUIET, SELF-CONTAINED PARTIES WITH BOOZE THAT WAS SMUGGLED IN. WE USED TO DISPOSE OF THE BOTTLES UNDER A LOOSE FLOOR BOARD IN THE OLD SAWMILL NEAR THE RIVER."

CLIFF PATON, RESEARCH

Workers at Lower Camp were transported via this DC-3 in the early 1960s.

over its decision, one reporter tried to capture the magnitude of the pilot operation with these words:

"An excavator, with a nine-foot diameter bucketwheel, is used to gnaw oil and sand loose from the hillside. The oil is separated from the sand in a weird-looking assembly of pipes, tanks and towers called an extraction unit. From 20 to 50 tons of oil sands material per hour is dumped into the unit, flushed with hot water and agitated. A black froth, containing oil, water and some solids is recovered."

While the reporter was clearly impressed with the magnitude of the operation, the Conservation Board was less so. The board conceded the experimental results produced by Cities Service were convincing. However,

concern was expressed that the market could not bear the increased volume of oil sands and still comply with a policy stating bituminous sands could not comprise more than five percent of total commercial oil production in Alberta.

Although the Conservation Board later granted a permit to Great Canadian Oil Sands, its deferral of the Cities Service's application dealt a near fatal blow to the Mildred Lake pilot project. In short order, the pilot plant was mothballed. Employees were laid off, equipment was stored. The dream became a nightmare and it was decided to concentrate research activities at the laboratory in Edmonton.

November 22, 1963, became known as "Black Friday" in the history annals of both Syncrude and the world.

COME FLY WITH ME

IN THE EARLY DAYS, A DC 3 WITH call letters CF-CUC journeyed through northern Alberta skies, carrying men and equipment. For many, the flight to the Mildred Lake site was their first airborne experience; air travel in the early sixties was still more the exception than the rule and it was a dizzying introduction to a whole new world.

The original pilot for Cities Service Athabasca Ltd. was Bob Hunter. A modern day adventurer, Hunter soon learned the location of every tree, lake and twig on the route.

Syncrude joined the age of high speed transportation in 1976 when the company purchased a King Air 100, a sporty, spiffy little craft that easily maintained the demanding schedule of two round trips daily.

Coordinating and scheduling passengers and flights proved a monumental task, but it was one handled with grace and ease by Ruby Harrison, who says the passenger roster numbered in the thousands over the years.

Keeping Syncrude's jet in top flying shape today are, from left: Marv Frederickson, Bill Fraser, Terry Vacheresse and Dale Henderson.

As the world mourned the assassination of U.S. President John F. Kennedy, a handful of men completed the shutdown, boarded the DC 3 and, as the primitive airstrip disappeared from view, wondered if they were seeing the site for the last time. The atmosphere was thick with tension and a feeling of disbelief.

Though the dream diminished, the vision endured. An old oxygen plant, on the eastern edge of Edmonton, was transformed in 1963 into a research laboratory. There, a semi-continuous unit capable of processing oil sand at a rate of 120 pounds per hour, was put into operation. Trucks full of oil sand made the journey to Edmonton over roads good-naturedly referred to as "rough"!

At the lab, geologists, engineers, planners and inventors took turns scooping the black gold onto conveyor belts, for transport to a miniature extraction plant.

In the words of George Williamson, the scene was one of rabid experimentation into unknown areas:

"The future fruit of all our toil
This country's huge reserves of oil
But what a sad unhappy nation
We used it all for experimentation!"

When he penned these lines at Syncrude's Edmonton Research facility in the late 1960s, Williamson was being only slightly facetious. Like the hundreds of scientists, technicians, engineers and support staff who have contrib-

uted to decades of Syncrude research history, he suspected there was something special about Syncrude's approach.

Few Canadian projects had ever undergone such concentrated investigation. At first, the push was on to develop and refine technology. Later, the focus switched to ongoing improvements throughout the operation.

The Cities Service Athabasca research laboratory in Edmonton. Circa 1964.

The research tradition is firmly rooted in Syncrude history. During the 1950s, while Cities Service Athabasca carried out pioneering research near Mildred Lake, other experiments were taking place in the Ontario laboratories of Imperial Oil Enterprises Ltd.

Imperial's Dr. Clem Bowman, who would later manage the Syncrude research program, was busily concocting a new bitumen extraction

Below: Cover text for a patent issued to Syncrude.

IT AIN'T HAY!!!

IT WAS LIKE STIRRING A CUBE OF SUGAR IN a cup of coffee — except that instead of adding a teaspoon, half a pound of oil sand had to be hefted into the research department's notorious Semi-Continuous Unit (SCU) for extraction every 15 seconds.

Assigned to minister to the SCU, a research staffer knew his biggest potential work hazard would be falling asleep and forgetting to feed the monster. The real danger in catching "40 winks" was that fellow workers would take the opportunity to paint your shoes different colors. In one case, the cleats on a modern-day Rip Van Winkle's shoes were even welded to the floor.

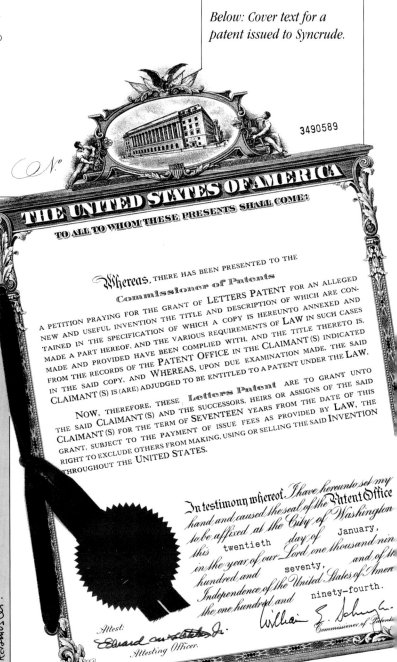

approach called the sand reduction process.

"I brought out a little pilot unit in 1962 and reassembled it at Mildred Lake. For a month it ran parallel to the Cities Service unit. However, it didn't perform very well on some feedstocks so a decision was made to stick to the hot water process."

Undeterred, Bowman returned to Sarnia and decided to learn all he could

about the hot water approach for extraction pioneered by the Alberta Research Council's Dr. Karl Clark. When Clark's results all checked out upon re-examination, Bowman admits he was "surprised that some of Clark's findings hadn't been embodied in the early Cities Service Athabasca pilot plant program."

Over the years, the extraction process was painstakingly reworked and reexamined to

include both proven principles and a few innovative twists. And when the gigantic extraction units finally rumbled into action, everyone agreed the years of research had finally paid off.

If extraction was the main focus of Syncrude research at the outset, the picture would soon expand to include environmental investigations, research in upgrading, and froth treatment experiments.

Researchers would concentrate as well on developing the improved lubricants, rubber technologies and space-age metals that keep the mine producing under often cruelly punishing climatic and operating conditions.

Though research's approach is seldom linear, the findings have quickly translated into plant improvements and productivity gains.

Drilling being carried out at Lower Camp to test the oil sand quality. Circa 1964.

When will the research phase be over? "Never," predicts Thane Waldie, vice-president, technology. "Every time you build something new, you present yourself with an opportunity to improve it. For example, the Capacity Addition Project in the 1980s gave us more upgrading capacity and that places tremendous pressure on extraction. Suddenly we face another research challenge!"

Mr. Invention — Luba Cymbalisty of research has been with the company for more than 25 years. During that time, he has secured 41 patents for the development of oil sands technology.

"GETTING BACK TO YOUR ROOTS"

THOUGH ONE WOULDN'T EXPECT to find a root cellar on the Syncrude inventory list, from 1961 until 1963, there was one. Getting year round oil sands to satisfy the enormous appetite of the research department was not easily accomplished during the long, bitter winters.

One gifted geologist, a farm boy at heart, hit on the idea of using a root cellar to keep the oil sands from freezing. It worked for potatoes, so why not?

Soon, a huge root cellar large enough to take a front-end loader, was constructed near the main road during the summer. Trees were razed, four feet of top soil supplied the insulation, and hundreds of tonnes of sand was hauled into the hole before freeze up.

Over the winter, the oil sand was shuttled out for processing. The results of the first batch were fine, but each succeeding load led to poorer results... and no one could understand why.

After superb sleuthing and extensive testing, it was discovered the root cellar was so warm and cozy, it created a perfect atmosphere for oil sands to oxidize and age!

The first bridge to allow access to the oil sands was built in 1964 by Great Canadian Oil Sands Limited (now Suncor).

Once the Mildred Lake pilot project ceased operations, the four major shareholders took another look at their plans. They decided to regroup and rethink their strategies. As 1964 came to a close, it looked like the project was sinking into a quicksand of delay and despair.

Fortunately, this prognosis was premature and like a regenerating phoenix, Syncrude would soon rise from the ashes.

Imperial Oil called in their top guns to surmount the obstacles...Frank Spragins and Dr. Clem Bowman, men known for their intuitive brilliance and perseverance, were both deeply committed to the success of the project and anxious to see it launched.

On December 18, 1964, Syncrude Canada Ltd. was incorporated. A month later, on January 1, 1965, Syncrude became the operator of the $16 million project. Its four original owners were: Imperial Oil Limited, Richfield Oil Corporation, Cities Service Athabasca, Inc. and Royalite Oil Company, Limited.

Rightfully, the man sitting in the president's chair and the first shareholder, was Frank Spragins, vanguard and visionary, a man strong enough to let his gentle nature show and stubborn enough to persevere against all odds.

From the head office, Spragins lobbied vigorously for his company, urging the government not to cause unnecessary delay in the development of the oil sands. He warned that if they waited

Transfers of the shares represented by this Certificate are on transfer as contained in the Articles of Association of S day of January, A. D., 1965.

NUMBER 1

SYNCRUDE

This Certifies that _____ F. K. Spragins

One

transferable only on the books of t person or by Attorney upon surrend

IN WITNESS WHEREOF, the said Corpo by its duly authorized officer this_____

Director

CERTIFICATE FOR SHARES of the Capital Stock

ISSUED TO

DATE

SHARES

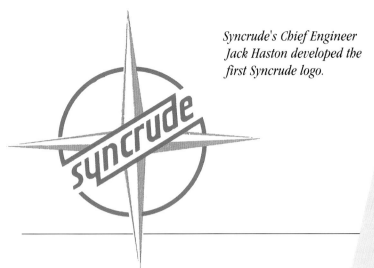
Syncrude's Chief Engineer Jack Haston developed the first Syncrude logo.

the rights of other shareholders and to the restriction
anada Ltd. and in the Participants' Agreement of the 1st

The first share in Syncrude Canada Ltd. was issued to its first President Frank Spragins.

too long, oil sand would be replaced by alternate sources, such as oil from shale in the United States. Spragins predicted that an oil shortage was coming and saw enormous potential in the sticky, oily sands of northern Alberta.

Since 1963, there had been several studies which made oil sands projects seem more feasible and therefore more attractive. In light of this new information, the Syncrude management committee began lobbying the provincial government to change its oil sands policy. The four partici-

pants had to decide if they wanted to continue with the project. It had already cost approximately $24 million and they still did not have government approval to begin construction.

Syncrude submitted several briefs to Alberta's Premier Ernest Manning which, together with submissions from other companies and associations, led to a new oil sands policy being tabled in the Legislative Assembly on February 20, 1968.

The battle for the oil sands would begin in earnest...

TAR BABY

WHILE FRANK Spragins and his colleagues lobbied vigorously for Syncrude's future on the home front, another group of oil sands enthusiasts, in owners' offices from Toronto to Tulsa, made their own forceful case. Having invested millions in research and preparation, they weren't about to let the Syncrude dream die without a struggle.

At shareholders' meetings and cocktail parties, in corporate boardrooms, business conferences and government offices, they never missed an opportunity to put in a plug for oil sands development, often beaming their message at those who knew little or nothing about Northern Alberta's massive resource.

Faced with a wealth of investment opportunities (most of which were deemed "safer" than oil sands mining and refining) and confronted with seemingly endless roadblocks to project approval, these multinational corporate players might easily have abandoned the project. The fact they continued is due in large part to the faith of influential boosters such as Cities Services' Dick Galbreath, Imperial's Jack Armstrong and Gulf's Floyd Aaring.

"One reason we hung in there, despite all the setbacks, is we knew the resource was there," says Galbreath, retired Cities Service vice president. "We didn't have to hunt for it — and that was a huge incentive."

His personal motives for pushing the Syncrude project went even further. "I had never heard of the oil sands until 1961 — but once I saw what was up there, I was hooked. I used to tell people my story was like the old Uncle Remus tale about the fox and the rabbit. Br'er Fox was always after Br'er Rabbit — until Br'er Rabbit smartened up and rigged up a tar baby. When Br'er Fox started slapping that tar baby around, he got stuck tight. For me, that's the Athabasca Tar Sands. It's the tar baby and it's stuck to me for life!"

As General Manager of production in Western Canada, and later President and Chief Executive Officer of Imperial Oil, Jack Armstrong also found it tough to resist the lure of the oil sands. "The Syncrude project just seemed like the right thing to do. My attitude was: we had the research, it looked like it would work, we had the money together, so why not go for it?"

When it turned out that "going for it" wouldn't be quite as straightforward as everyone had hoped, many oil patch observers predicted the joint venture partners would soon lose interest and simply walk away.

Floyd Aaring, former Gulf

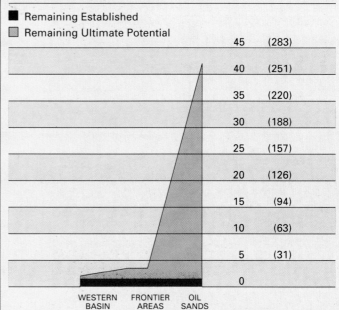

Crude Oil Reserves in Canada
Billion Cubic Metres (Barrels)

■ Remaining Established
▨ Remaining Ultimate Potential

45	(283)	
40	(251)	
35	(220)	
30	(188)	
25	(157)	
20	(126)	
15	(94)	
10	(63)	
5	(31)	
0		

WESTERN BASIN   FRONTIER AREAS   OIL SANDS

Estimates carried out by the Energy Resources Concervation Board indicate that 5.2 million cubic metres (33 billion barrels) of bitumen are potentially recoverable through surface mining.

FRANK SPRAGINS

vice president, admits it was sometimes difficult to keep up morale.

"The mood of the owner companies changed many times for better or for worse during the trials and tribulations of attempting to undertake such a huge and costly project in the face of seeming adversity."

Critics who expected the venture to fall apart in the face of constant delays and economic concerns, obviously didn't understand the owners' expectations.

According to Aaring, "the owners didn't see this as a gold mine but as a potentially profitable venture. Little new conventional oil was being discovered and so it was a plan for long-term energy supply for Alberta and Canada."

Armstrong agrees. "You have to remember that crude oil prices were not that high — somewhere around $2 a barrel — when we committed to Syncrude. It certainly wasn't planned with the expectation we would get $75 a barrel or anything close to that."

"YOUR OLD MEN SHALL
DREAM DREAMS; YOUR
YOUNG MEN SHALL SEE
VISIONS."

THE OLD TESTAMENT
JOEL 2:28

HIS WIFE REMEMBERS him as a good man, a quiet, gentle soul with a single-minded intensity that was virtually all consuming. He was a man with the courage of his convictions and the resilience only a deeply committed individual can bring to a mission.

The deep convictions that Frank Spragins brought to the long, laborious and often arduous battle for the right to develop Alberta's oil sands has made his name synonymous with "Syncrude". Spragins, the first president and chief executive officer of a company that changed the nature of the Alberta economy and earned the province a world-class reputation as a producer of black gold, devoted a substantial part of his adult life to bringing substance to a dream.

Born in Mississippi and

educated at Rice University in Houston, Spragins started his career with Carter Oil, a subsidiary of Standard Oil of New Jersey.

In 1942, he responded to his country's call for men to come forward and defend their country. Spragins wanted to join the armed services, but the War Office had other plans for the young, electrical engineer. They felt he could be more effective if he continued his search for oil, in either South America or Canada. Spragins chose Canada and

moved to Alberta the same year. Although he had no way of knowing it at the time, his life's work was underway.

Always at the forefront, Spragins was a member of

Frank Spragins' dream, now a reality, went into production in 1978.

Syncrude opening ceremonies in September 1978.

temporary irritants to be overcome. Soon, he took on the sometimes tedious task of dealing with governments to fight for the right to develop the Syncrude complex. At the same time he was also engaged in "damming the high wall", shoring up the confidence of investors.

In 1964, Spragins was to assume the presidency of the newly-created Syncrude Canada Ltd. (a combination of the words synthetic and crude). After its construction, he would become chairman of the board.

Even dreamers must eventually look to new frontiers and in late 1977, Frank Spragins announced his retirement. Although few realized it, the most vocal and visible proponent of oil sands development in Alberta was in failing health. At the official opening of the $2.3 billion plant, Spragins was "embraced" by a crowd of more than 700 people. Their standing ovation was public

the geophysical team that discovered oil in Leduc, a find that started the northern Alberta oil boom. Then working for Standard's Canadian affiliate, Imperial Oil, in the Athabasca Tar Sands department, Spragins was identified as a man who could make the government come round to his way of thinking.

John Barr, former Syncrude director of public affairs explains: "Frank Spragins had this incredible political astuteness. It wasn't just his ability to deal with governments. There were times when he kept the project alive by

playing one owner off against the others.

"He admitted that when any of the partners began to falter in their resolve to stay with the project, he would say 'that's too bad because such and such a partner is really excited about this.' Then the others would wonder what that company knew that they didn't — and they'd all decide to hang in for a while longer."

The determination and perseverance he'd learned growing up without a father stood him in good stead for the next decade. He ignored negative responses and viewed obstacles in his path as

Hot on the Hoof:
What to do in terms of land reclamation? Syncrude has considered planting grass instead of trees . . . then sitting back and watching both bitumen and beef bring in the BUCKS.

acknowledgment of his dedication and conviction.

"It took 19 years for Frank to witness his moment of victory," says his wife Eleanor (Nell) Spragins. "He had a dream, a vision, and he devoted his heart, life and soul to it. I'm eternally grateful he was there to see Syncrude up and running."

Frank Spragins, the man behind the mission and a visionary of the first order, died six weeks after the official opening of the Syncrude operation.

Government played a critical role in the development of the oil sands. Legislation in those early days, though not prohibitive, was certainly restrictive. Syncrude, along with a number of other major companies and professional associations, vigorously negotiated with government, asking politicians and civil servants to reconsider and rewrite policies. Eventually, their persistence paid off. In February, 1968, the Legislative Assembly tabled a new oil sands policy and changed the course of economic history in the province of Alberta.

MEMBERS OF THE COUNTRY CLUB

IT WAS 1965. Hippies were swarming to Haight-Ashbury. Peace and love were common themes in music... and everyone was caught up in the struggle for equal rights.

At Syncrude, the battle for equality was settled, at least on one front, by the creation of the Syncrude Social Society (SSS), an offshoot of the Doherty Mens' Fraternity.

The goal of the Syncrude Social Society was to promote fellowship through leisure programs and activities for all Syncrude employees and their families.

During its 25 year history, the SSS, staffed by volunteers and supported financially by the company as well as employees, has been responsible for the coordination and execution of literally hundreds of picnics, barbecues, dances and sporting events.

Today, the SSS hosts the largest lobster boil in Canada, serving approximately 6,300 lobsters. The annual Christmas celebration also draws hundreds of children of all ages, for treats, treasures and the pure pleasure of greeting Santa Claus.

Syncrude Social Society Christmas parties are the highlight of the year for many employees' children.

IT'S A GO!

2

A new oil sands policy increasing total combined output limits on both plants to 150,000 barrels per day was only the first step on the lengthy path leading to development of the oil sands industry. In May 1968, Syncrude's application to build a $200 million plant, able to produce 80,000 barrels daily, was before the Energy Resources Conservation Board. However, the application faltered in light of an unexpected development.

Huge oil reserves, apparently enough to create a surplus of conventional oil, were discovered in Alaska!

The government hedged, taking a "wait and see" attitude, anxious to determine what impact the Prudhoe Bay find would have on the conventional oil market. A new hearing was set for a year later.

The company reeled in shock. But the patience of the owners was remarkable. They reapplied. The application was again deferred. Eventually, it became abundantly clear the future of the oil sands was governed by forces beyond the owners' control.

They were bewildered.

But before they could fully recover from the shock, an explosion and fire rocked the research facility in the spring of 1968. In an shed separate from the laboratory, tests were being conducted by running bitumen through a heated salt bath. Something happened to the temperature control and the metal shed blew up. Miraculously, no one was injured but there was extensive damage to an adjoining building. The future once again looked grim as an overpowering sense of misgiving rippled through the company.

The strain was beginning to show on everyone, including Frank Spragins. He sent a terse and powerful message to

Having supplies on hand is crucial to the reliability of the company's operations. This photo was taken in the central maintenance shop.

the government, saying "...we are finding it exceedingly difficult, both individually and jointly to continue financial support for oil sand development without definite forseeable goals. We must emphasize that any additional substantial delay may well have the same effect as a denial of application."

Spragins' ultimatum must have had an impact. The government offered a truce, if not a peace treaty, saying it would consider another application.

A long, hot summer of waiting followed the May, 1969 hearing. The tension was obvious, but Frank Spragins was confident. Intuitive and optimistic, he felt the moment he had long awaited was near at hand: It was.

On September 12, 1969, the Energy Resources Conservation Board authorized Syncrude to build a plant with 80,000 barrels per day capacity not to go on stream before July 1, 1976. (It was later decided the start up date had to be amended to 1978. In the end, the company's permit was amended to allow it to produce 129,400 barrels per day.)

Nearly a decade of waiting, debating, floundering and faltering were over. With approval in place, the dream finally had substance. However, despite the fact construction approvals had been issued, the war to build the mammoth project was only beginning.

It would take until September 18, 1973, for Premier Peter Lougheed to announce the government had reached a final agreement with Syncrude to build a $1 billion plant, with the ability to produce 80,000 barrels of crude daily, in northeastern Alberta's Oil Sand Country!

A New Dawn

IT WAS THE END OF YEARS of waiting, indecision and fragmentation. The moment had finally come, but the reception room in Edmonton's Corona Hotel seemed wrapped in a time warp. There was a sense of quiet optimism lavishly mixed with disbelief. After all, there had been a steady succession of deferments. Maybe this was just a hoax, another false lead, another major disappointment. After all, they'd been close before and just when they thought they were on a roll, approval was withheld.

The room, equipped with television sets, was almost quiet; conversation was subdued, adding to the dreamlike quality of the moment.

Frank Spragins sat at the back of the room, isolated in his own thoughts, no doubt wondering if the end was at hand or if this was just another chapter in the licensing nightmare.

Finally, Premier Peter Lougheed's face filled the screens. His voice said the words they'd been waiting to hear, and confirmed what the owners had known for a few days. The Alberta government had completed an agreement with Syncrude to build a $1 billion plant.

Syncrude was finally a go!

A cheer went up from the crowd. Frank Spragins smiled a tired smile, one that betrayed the toll the years of seemingly endless haggling had taken. The media described the long struggle, to obtain the endorsement and support of the government, as "... the hardest fought dogfight of the oil industry in modern times."

SUNCOR:
OIL SANDS PIONEER

THE PIONEERING spirit was rich and strong in the early days of commercial oil sands development. It was a risky venture at best and much of the technology was either brand new or waiting to be discovered.

In 1967, in the midst of Syncrude's bargaining and bartering with government, Great Canadian Oil Sands Limited (GCOS), now Suncor, built the first oil sands plant in the world and began to produce oil. Grappling with new, emerging technologies and a host of unforseen operational headaches, the GCOS facility initially produced 12,000 barrels of synthetic crude oil daily.

An overview of Suncor, the world's first oil sands plant, built near Fort McMurray, Alberta.

During the application phase, every triumph was followed by a numbing disaster, every disaster by a ray of light. But the spirit and doggedness of the oil sand pioneers was renewed with the government's approval to forge ahead.

The glue binding the men and women of the oil sands together was their youth, ambition, vitality and energy. They had faith enough to move mountains of indecision and approached the construction of the Syncrude plant with an enthusiasm usually reserved for affairs of the heart.

What they did not know, or apparently did not realize, was they were creating a true giant, a phenomenon of worldwide importance.

The gestation period for getting construction approval had been demanding and difficult but the real labor to build a $1 billion baby was only just beginning! Work began almost immediately.

The same rivers and water systems that provided a living and a means for transportation for settlers a century before, now at-

Right: In the fall of 1973, work began at Syncrude. This photo shows the cleared area at the site of the present tailings pond.

Below: The Poplar Creek spillway after completion.

In 1975, work was underway on the Poplar Creek spillway.

tracted a new kind of entrepreneur — one interested in harvesting the bounty of the oil sands. Unlike their forebears, these new pioneers had to redirect nature for their purpose.

The first, and in someway, most formidable task was to clear the site. An archaeological dig, to prevent the destruction of artifacts in the area was undertaken in 1973. Over 900 artifacts were recovered, including stone fragments which were probably the result of early humans making tools.

Archeologists concluded that a site which Syncrude discovered on the banks of Beaver Creek had been used as a limestone quarry. This site was subsequently designated as a provincial historic resource in recognition of its importance to the understanding of the history of early man in the region. Later, a $28 million dollar diversion to divert the water from the mine was carried out. The course of Beaver Creek was rerouted with two earthen dams and a large concrete spillway. Two new bridges, each with a load capacity of 450 tonnes were constructed over the Athabasca River and Poplar Creek.

A fleet of buses, used to transport thousands of constuction workers to and from the site, was retained.

During the course of construction, more than $2 billion dollars was doled out for materials, equipment and labor.

A tributary of Beaver Creek.

The volume of materials required to build the mammoth operation gave a whole new dimension to the meaning of "buying in bulk". During construction, more than 500,000 tons of stores, equipment, vessels and plant components were trucked to Fort McMurray on Highway 63, a route that could, in kindest terms, be described as "nearly impassable." Since hundreds of loads were excessive in weight and dimension, they required detailed planning comparable to the well-timed choreography of the Royal Canadian Mounted Police's Musical Ride.

At one point, the movement of large equipment became a major nuisance to Fort McMurrayites. They were, understandably, more than a little distressed with large chunks of heavy equipment or pieces of pipe falling off transport trucks and blocking traffic! Fortunately, patience and a collective sense of humor about the situation prevailed.

The Syncrude construction project continued to break new ground. Almost daily, both literally and figuratively, new precedents were set.

The foundations for the fluid cokers were poured and a huge dome, supported by air, was raised to shield construction workers from the winter weather, as they laid the foundation for the plant. A 600 foot smokestack was raised and quickly earned acclaim as one of the tallest structures in the province.

During construction, there was constant activity. It was nail-biting time once again when 700 tonnes of equipment had to be eased over an Athabasca River bridge, so new it still lacked safety rails... The bridge held and so did the punishing construction schedule!

Notes Frank MacNamara, Bechtel procurement manager: "There were so many records associated with this job — the two biggest cokers ever built, construction of the two biggest reformer furnaces, reactors that were then the heaviest vessels ever to move into Western Canada. In all, we moved 1.1 million tonnes of material for the job."

In Edmonton, Bechtel's Fred Britton faced his own "mission impossible" overseeing frantic activity at module yards and unsnarling the inevitable glitches.

"In hindsight, we think it went very well but certainly we had our problems. It was especially tough to find construction equipment

A view of constuction activity in secondary upgrading.

Right: Assembly of a giant dragline. Circa 1977.

Left: The 600 ft. smokestack under construction in July, 1975.

Trucking was a big factor in securing the equipment for construction.

because there was so much construction activity going on in North America at the time." This would include such major projects as Expo '67.

Syncrude Construction Manager John Lynn didn't envy Bechtel's challenge. "I still shudder when I think of some of the requests that went out to the procurement people — 'We need another five 200-tonne cranes — tomorrow!' Some of us had never even seen a 200 tonne crane — but Bechtel would scour the countryside and somehow come up with them."

Lynn is convinced the project put a new twist on the traditional owner/contractor relationship. "It's generally adversarial. But in this case, the job was so big, we knew we'd simply have to find a way to work to-gether. We did, and it paid off for all of us."

"THERE WAS CONSIDERABLE ANXIETY DURING THE BUILDUP BECAUSE OF THE SIZE AND NATURE OF THE PROJECT AND CONCERNS AROUND PROVIDING LODGING AND TRANSPORTATION FOR SUCH A LARGE WORKPLACE. . .

SPECIAL LEGISLATION WAS PASSED TO PROVIDE A SITE AGREEMENT FOR THE MILDRED LAKE PROJECT. THIS LIFTED THE PROJECT OUT OF A PROVINCIAL BARGAINING SITUATION SO THERE WOULD BE NO STRIKES OR LOCKOUTS DURING CONSTRUCTION. AS A RESULT, BECHTEL NEGOTIATED WITH ALL OF THE TRADES FOR A COMMON AGREEMENT SURROUND-ING WORK CONDITIONS.

BERNIE SMYTH
LABOUR RELATIONS

By mid-1972, Syncrude staff still numbered less than 100 but the recruitment rush was about to begin. Dave Pogue, representing one half the staff of a fledgling employee relations group, recalls early efforts to pull together benefit packages and employee programs ahead of the onslaught.

"All of our programs tended to be leading edge stuff. And, of course, management knew they would have to pay quite well to get the best people — especially since working conditions weren't always the greatest."

He recalls engineers and construction specialists streaming on to the site. They came from countries as far

afield as Uganda, the Philippines, Holland, Australia, Japan, and Chile. It was the first wave of an international recruiting drive that would see Syncrude staff double in each of the next five years.

"Many of the people who came for the construction phase weren't the kind to opt for a stable employment environment. They liked to do a job and move on to the next project. Some were wildly imaginative, some terribly demanding. They were attracted by the fact that to a large degree they were able to use independent judgment.

They were given "the green light" — and, happily, most succeeded.

"These were people with strong personalities and what welded them together was the challenge of the project."

Surprisingly, many of these one-time industrial nomads decided to stay on after construction. Pogue suspects they knew they had experienced something special and were reluctant to let it go. "After being associated with something so big and so important, they wanted to stick around and see the rest of the story unfold."

If contractors were facing many challenges and changes, so were many new employees. For most new employees, a job at Syncrude meant "heading North". But for a small minority, it meant moving south to milder weather, bright lights and big city amenities.

Ann Culliton's previous Canadian experience was confined to the northern hydro projects which had attracted her engineer husband. "Here I was in a place with a traffic light . . . with a road out . . . with stores. I could get a

Syncrude's workforce is both highly-skilled and cosmopolitan. People from around the world were recruited to work on the project.

THE POPULATION BOMB

DURING THE 1970S, THE COMMUNITY of Fort McMurray became vibrant, charged with life. The population doubled, tripled, quadrupled with dramatic speed. The formerly out-of-the-way northern community suddenly developed its own international flavor as people from throughout the province, across the country and around the world brought their histories, cultures and customs to Alberta's north.

Cultures and customs from around the world flourish in Fort McMurray.

driver's license. It was wonderful!"

Similarly, while southerners complained of cabin fever during northern Alberta winters, facilities maintenance's Dennis King had no such complaint. "I had just come from the Arctic — so this seemed like the sunny south."

King was born and raised in Alberta and had spent a number of years in the Yukon until the lure of Syncrude drew him like a magnet "... back south; I guess I was ready to come home again. But when I got here, I was amazed! There were only a handful of people from Alberta... every other person you met was from somewhere else, and I don't mean just other parts of Canada although there were plenty of those, but from the United States, England, Ireland, Italy, Portugal... everywhere."

Fort McMurray's population created a rich blend of cultures, a truly Canadian mosaic. Grocery stores diversified their standard fare to accommodate different eating habits. Pungent eastern spices shared shelves with maritime favorites such as fiddlehead greens and dried cod.

According to Paul Tichinoff, former loss management

executive, "... there was a time when Fort McMurray was known as the third largest city in Newfoundland!"

Cultural events celebrated the differences in cultures while they respected, honored and valued the profound contributions that individuals brought with them. And a whole new language began to emerge. The sayings of one group became the everyday vocabulary of others. Colorful expressions such as: "Up to your axles in mud" became a testimony to rough road conditions and "slope rats" was an expressive term used to describe the men who maneuvered machines over rough terrain. "Stay where you're at till I come where you're to!" and "Are you from the bay, boy?" also began to roll off the tongues of many, regardless of their roots!

Tatsu Horiuchi, one of the employees on loan from Japan, assisted in the plant start up.

A part of the original plant, the 15-2 gas oil hydrotreater is being transported to site in modular form. Circa 1976.

A BETTER IDEA

The tub of the dragline.

INNOVATION WAS THE NAME OF the game on site as engineers by the hundreds, and planners and technicians encountered new and unusual problems every day. The stories of creativity and originality in overcoming difficulties are classic; the solutions to the problems often beautiful in their simplicity.

In 1977, a mammoth dragline tub had to be jacked up on piles during construction to enable work to be completed underneath it. Once this was finished, engineers faced the "weighty problem" of how to lower it to the ground. A great deal of discussion ensued as to how the feat would best be accomplished without spending many hours and halting further construction.

A young mechanical engineer from Bechtel, named Wayne O'Grady, suggested six tons of ice be placed under the 900 ton dragline tub, and as the ice melted, which ice is prone to do, the tub would simply end up resting on the ground.

Despite the skepticism of his peers, who were concerned the ice would crack from the weight and bring the tub crashing to the ground, the engineer conducted his experiment and had the last laugh. It worked!

At one point more than 800 engineers were at work on the project — piecing together a technological puzzle in offices from Edmonton, Calgary and Vancouver to San Francisco and Houston. The final tally showed more than two-thirds of the project was engineered in Canada.

All of this had a major impact on the capacity and reputation of the Canadian engineering sector.

Terry Allen, retired senior executive with Canadian Occidental Petroleum and longtime member of the Syncrude management committee, looks back today on the wave of Canadian nationalism that surfaced in the days following Syncrude approval.

"There were fears among Canadian engineers they would

The plant 10 control centre and the water treatment plant during construction. Circa 1976.

A dragline is a massive mining machine with a bucket the size of a two-car garage.

We Are The Engineers

SYNCRUDE'S TRADITION OF engineering excellence is anchored in the earliest Royalite and Cities Service research activities at Mildred Lake.

One pilot plant employee remembers the atmosphere: "Engineers like Ron Gray were pretty sharp. They had plenty of questions — and we soon learned it wasn't a bad idea to have the right answers."

Over the years, these "sons of Martha" reveled in the challenges: establishing the design basis for the plant, choosing the mine location, setting the stage for the extraction, froth treatment and bitumen upgrading processes, and designing everything from bridges to spillways.

When things calmed down, someone added up the figures and announced the initial project had generated "3.5 million technical person hours" worth of conceptual design, engineering, procurement, and project management services. What that meant, said one observant, but nontechnical type, is "one heck of a lot of engineering effort." So much in fact, that Syncrude and Suncor are now counted among the top 10 Canadian engineering achievements of the century.

be crowded out by huge American firms. In the end, of course, this didn't happen."

Since then, Canadian engineering content in such areas as plant improvements and additions has mushroomed.

Says Allen, "A lot of the engineering knowledge and capacity resulting from the initial Syncrude project has remained in Alberta and Canada and that's great."

In the mid-1960s, youthful engineers in search of exciting and rewarding careers tended to scoop up their Canadian degrees and quickly head south of the border.

It was about this time that Al Hyndman, now general manager, development, decided he ought to be able to put his newly-earned chemical engineering degree to work in Western Canada. The best bet for that, he decided, was clearly the oil sands and most particularly, the fledgling Syncrude venture.

Left: Engineering staff at Syncrude. Standing L. to R.: James M. Hay, Jay Petigara, Azamul Kahrim, Mike Sneath. Bottom row L. to R.: Rajinder Sehdev, Patricia Dutchak, Karen Gable.

The tank farm area prior to tank construction. Circa 1975.

"It was different, it was new, it was big, and it was hard to do. In short, Syncrude was a dream for an engineer."

Over the past quarter century, Hyndman and literally thousands of his counterparts, both Syncrude employees and consultants, have had a chance to live the dream.

As Thane Waldie, vice president, technology, puts it, "This has always been an

Al Hyndman.

exciting training ground for young engineers. They learn a hell of a lot in a very short time."And even in relatively stable times the company continues to replace the 50 or so "10 year veterans" who routinely move on every year. The only difference is today, more and more members of the 850 member engineering and technical staff are women.

JUMPING THE CONSTRUCTION HURDLES

A QUICK GLANCE AT THE Syncrude site in 1975 might have left the impression that the Bechtel organization was the oil sands' newest corporate player.

Outnumbering Syncrude personnel 10 to one, Bechtel forces —including people from their refinery, power, mining and pipeline divisions — had calmly moved into the site and set up shop, doing what they had done countless times before. They were preparing to turn out yet another frontier resource project with skill, confidence — and to some in the tiny cadre of Syncrude overseers — a generous helping of arrogance.

The men at the top of the Syncrude organization, President Brent Scott and Project Manager C. R. "Chuck" Collyer, had worked with Bechtel on earlier projects and respected the enormous capability and technical strength

A ROOM WITH A VIEW

AN OFFICE WITH a view, or even a window, was a rarity to be cherished on the Syncrude site during the 70 s. Alex Sawers, cost specialist and material co-ordinator, quickly learned this when he joined the shutdown crew and found himself holed up in a windowless cubbyhole.

"Eventually, they decided to locate shutdown personnel in trailers. I inspected my new office and found I had six windows. I was ecstatic — but my joy was short-lived. Pretty soon they stuck trailers on each side of mine. I still had my windows — and a view six inches to the units next door."

Air conditioners were also a scarce and highly prized item, Sawers remembers. "You could leave your office at night with the air conditioner going full blast. In the morning, you'd be greeted by a hole in the wall and a stifling office."

A common sight during constuction of the Syncrude project was a maze of cranes dominating the skyline.

Sections of the major vessels of a coker awaiting assembly.

of the San Francisco-based contractor.

Other Syncrude staffers remember constantly struggling to establish some sort of identity against the well-oiled Bechtel machine.

Said one, "It was our job to keep looking over Bechtel's shoulder to make sure we got our money's worth. But there were so few of us at the time — something like 80 of us and 800 of them — it was kind of like the tail trying to wag the dog. I can tell you, that was some big dog!"

Despite early uneasiness in the relationship, the crushing pressure of schedules and budgets soon brought owners, Syncrude management and Bechtel representatives together in an atmosphere of cooperation and mutual respect.

Frank MacNamara, Bechtel procurement manager for the job says Syncrude was one of the biggest projects Bechtel had taken on up to that time. "Certainly it was one of the most complex."

He remembers a lot of tight squeaks — like the time a train derailed in Saskatchewan and left 30 carloads of dragline components sprawled across a farmer's field. "In a case like that you simply go out and get them rebuilt — and keep a sharp eye on the calendar while you're doing it."

THERE'S NO LIFE LIKE IT

A LOT OF WORKERS were coming and going during construction, but none arrived with such drama as the Canadian Armed Forces. About 900 paratroopers literally dropped into the Mildred Lake area during a training session. One of the few women in the area at the time was heard to say: ". . . it was magnificent to see but we really didn't need a lot more men up in the area at the time."

John Culliton remembers helping the army pick out the drop site.

"I gave them a tour in late March and they chose a flat area south of Beaver Creek. They didn't realize it was on top of muskeg and, vindictive little devil that I am, I didn't tell them what that would mean in summer. One of the paratroopers said to me later, 'The jump? Oh that was wonderful — but the landing left me in crap up to my shoulders!'"

"IT'S IN THE MAIL"

CANADA POST made major contributions to the project in its own way. Despite the company's near global renown, more than one individual had difficulty determining just how to get the mail through. Letters were sent (and to Canada Post's credit, eventually delivered!) to the following addresses:

- A. Hewett, SCL, Edmonton, Albama
- Syncreed Con Ltd, Syncrude Alberta, North Canada
- Tarzans, Fort McMurray, Alberta
- Athabasca Oil Sands, Alberta

During the recruitment stage, one letter clearly indicated the writer, a Canadian, was confused by all the activity in the oil industry! It read (sic):

"Dear Sir:
I recently saw your advertisement and I am consider looking abroad for work. I would like you to send any further information you have on your company and also any information you might have on the Mackenzie pipeline project."

CONSTRUCTION FEVER

3

Construction was well underway, but there was still a great deal of fear and uncertainty. In December 1974, the fragility of the project was once again underscored when Atlantic Richfield, one of the four original owners, withdrew financial support. The withdrawal was likely influenced by high inflation which had essentially doubled the cost of the project from the initial construction estimates.

For more than two months, the entire Syncrude organization existed in a state of suspended animation, until the governments of Alberta and Canada intervened.

Syncrude's cokers are the world's largest, easily dwarfing the truck in the foreground of the picture. Circa 1976.

AS WE LIKE IT

WINTER AT SYNCRUDE SEEMED even longer than usual that year. With Atlantic Richfield out of the game and no corporate successor in sight to save the day, employees faced what might have been the final days of their Syncrude careers.

Lesser souls might have quaked under the pressure. Syncrude staffers chose to party. In fact they chose to party with class. Somehow the gravity of the situation ruled out a casual beer and pretzels affair. The first GO/NO GO party clearly called for something more culturally uplifting.

Suddenly, out from behind desks, out from under hard hats emerged a full-fledged troupe of Shakespearean actors. Seasoned in the theatre (they had had at least one rehearsal) they overwhelmed their audience with their sensitive interpretation of the classic "Hamit As You Like It."

Irreverently adapted from Shakespeare's original by John Culliton, the dramatic offering obviously dazzled the audience and left critics groping for words (or was it the door?).

It had all the elements of a Hollywood thriller. In late January 1975, a Calgary oil executive flew into Winnipeg, booked 30 rooms for unnamed guests at the International Inn, then quietly headed for home, knowing the stage was set for one of the most economically and politically significant government-industry encounters in Canada's history.

By February 3, Calgary's Bill Mooney, Cities Service President, was back at the International Inn, quietly ticking off names on his list of mystery guests. Despite punishing schedules and relatively short notice, they had all arrived at the appointed time.

Two influential federal cabinet ministers, two provincial premiers and the heads of four powerful multinational corporations led the procession. For each key player, there was a cadre of prominent support troops — deputy ministers, senior executives, assorted economists, lawyers and policy advisers.

What had brought this high powered group to Winnipeg? It was perceived as neutral ground for a meeting that would decide the fate of the expansive — and by now shockingly expensive —

Syncrude Canada Ltd. project in Alberta's Athabasca Oil Sands.

The whole venture had been shaky for months. It started with revelations in late 1974 that project costs were wildly escalating; costs had more than doubled — to around $2 billion.

Then one of the original backers of the deal, Atlantic Richfield, pulled out of the venture, leaving a discouraging

Chuck Collyer

30 percent gap in project financing. The remaining owners, Imperial Oil, Gulf Canada and Cities Service, couldn't afford to continue on their own and a frantic two-month campaign to gain new private sector equity partners had proved unsuccessful.

Even for this group of gung-ho entrepreneurs, accustomed to the uncertain fortunes of

Research continues to improve and create new technology.

the oil patch, the future looked unusually gloomy.

As Imperial Oil Chairman Jack Armstrong would say later, "There was no doubt the whole thing could have gone down the drain. We stood to lose everything we had invested over the years."

By now the owners were facing other harsh realities. The consequences of pulling the pin on a project, which had clearly involved them emotionally as well as financially, were horrendous. Shutdown, they knew, would cost at least $250 million — a loss that would severely strain corporate

coffers and cause tense moments at upcoming shareholders' meetings.

Formidable lawsuits could ensue. The social and economic consequences — in terms of lost employment and business opportunities — would be painful for Alberta and for all of Canada. And finally, the defeat of Syncrude would almost surely deal a death blow to oil sands development, at least in the near term. Canada would clearly have to adjust its expectations regarding energy self-suffi-

ciency. Visions of a nation held hostage to the producers of Venezuela or the Persian Gulf began to emerge.

As these considerations and more whirled in the heads of participants, hotel staff scrambled to prepare the meeting room. A table long enough to accommodate each of the central players and their key advisers was set up. When Mooney saw the layout, he hastily called for a square table, a tiny act of diplomacy that ruled out any possibility of psychological one-upmanship

in the bargaining place.

By 9.30 a.m., on February 3, 1975, five delegations were in place. Representing the Government of Canada were Treasury Board's Jean Chretien and Energy Minister Donald Macdonald and their advisers. Premier Peter Loughheed headed the Alberta delegation while Premier Bill Davis led the Ontario contingent. Each was flanked by senior cabinet ministers. Representing Syncrude owners were R.V. (Bob) Sellers, chairman of Cities Service, Imperial Oil's Jack Armstrong and Gulf President J. A. (Jerry) McAfee.

The remaining chairs were reserved for Shell Canada Limited President Bill Daniel and his senior executives.

Preparing a float for a parade is part of the carpentry team's busy schedule.

AVAILABLE FUNDS IN TERMS OF DEBT — $ 400 m

COMMITTMENTS
GOV'TS
IOL   400 m
Gulf   625 m
Cities   325 m
             425 m   (125
SHORT?   >1775 m   (125
             150
             1925
SHORT   225
             75

400
250
150

Lymonde
Winnipeg Meeting
Feb 3/1975

The Winnipeg Agreement

However, Shell's presence at the table was short-lived. Considered the last hope for further private investment in the venture, Shell lost no time in making its intentions clear. The company might consider investing if the deal involved a guaranteed floor price for synthetic crude to minimize the risk should prices fall.

When this idea was rejected (government said "no" and the existing owners agreed they preferred to take their chances on prevailing world prices, good or bad), Daniel and his advisers withdrew.

The teams were now even — three corporate players, three government players.

Observers, recalling the ebb and flow of negotiations, later said proceedings ranged from "hot and heavy" to surprisingly informal. Jean Chretien commanded a flip chart, tracking the millions as investors and potential investors weighed risk against reward. At one point, delegates were huddled on the floor over a huge scrap of paper which made the making of a $2 billion project look deceptively simple. A few hundred million here, a few hundred million there — and presto a $2 billion project could be resurrected!

As totals were added, a shortfall of several million dollars remained. Armstrong recalls relaying a hastily written note from Gulf's Jerry McAfee to Sellers of Cities Service. It said, in effect: "If you'll take x million I'll take the rest and we'll have the thing sewn up."

Jack Armstrong, who had met Bill Davis at a cocktail party on the previous evening, had urged him jokingly to act as "honest broker between the 'Feds' and Alberta." (The two governments had been scrapping over future petrochemical developments and nerves on both sides were a trifle raw.)

Participants later agreed that Davis had indeed kept discussions on track, once suggesting to the government delegations they withdraw to "caucus" — which the oil company heads quickly translated to mean "cool off".

Dick Galbreath, who as Cities Service Vice President was also at the table, felt the Ontario government commitment to investing in Syncrude was a "bit shaky" at first.

"Before they signed, they wanted some kind of guarantee. Ultimately, everyone understood that if we went broke, we went broke together and they finally came around. Later on, of course, Ontario sold its interest at a profit."

The delegates had clearly come prepared to make decisions. Alberta had ordered an independent study of the

new Syncrude cost estimates. The results, presented to the meeting, showed the figures were both reliable and credible, based on inflation and on the more detailed picture of plant requirements which Bechtel Corporation, in charge of engineering, procurement and construction, and Syncrude had now been able to paint. (The fact that the project was completed within this budget would later prove their assessment correct.)

Both the oil companies and the Alberta government had also been doing their homework. During the weeks leading up to the Winnipeg Meeting, corporate executives had crisscrossed the country, furiously trying to crystallize government support behind the project. Alberta government ministers had been lobbying their counterparts in the federal and Ontario governments.

Royalty and tax concerns were not an issue. An agreement, which saw Alberta put aside normal royalties in favor of a 50/50 profit-sharing agreement with the Syncrude owners, had been hammered out months earlier. It had also been agreed the province would take a major ownership position in both the crude oil pipeline from the oil sands to

Edmonton and the utilities plant that would support the complex.

The corporate owners later admitted the deal established both Premier Lougheed and Don Getty, then Federal and Intergovernmental Affairs Minister, as tough and tenacious bargainers.

At the same time, Ottawa had made some tax concessions.

Soon, all of these details were confirmed. It was agreed as well that crude oil from Syncrude would sell at the international price and

no restrictions would be placed on production or sale.

Armstrong said later, "Eventually, everybody came up to a stalling point and at that point we reached some agreement. I would say we all got pretty much what we wanted."

What did everybody want? Analysts figured it this way. Lougheed wanted to secure the province's future as a major

energy player and ensure Albertans would benefit from development of their oil sands resource.

Davis wanted to tie up a long-term crude oil supply for Ontario and, in the meantime, gain a boost for the Ontario economy through lucrative Syncrude contracts.

For Canada, the goal was energy self-sufficiency. For the corporate players, the deal represented an opportunity to recover their hefty investment in Syncrude and keep alive their dream of pioneering in a

Threading the needle Syncrude style.

The bucketwheel is aligned with the conveyor belt in order to transfer oil sand.

field of energy development that was clearly the wave of the future.

By 9:30, that evening, the deal was set. Atlantic Richfield's 30 per cent interest would be replaced by Canada (15%), Alberta (10%) and Ontario (5%).

It was over — and all of the bargainers appeared satisfied. Then, as delegations began to withdraw, Dick Galbreath tugged at the sleeve of one of the lawyers present and questioned anxiously, "Shouldn't we get something down on paper?" Deals on a handshake might be the stuff of oil industry legend, but somehow this seemed a bit too important to leave to chance.

In the end, a scanty document outlining the principles of the agreement was signed by the six key participants — and one of the most unusual meetings in Canadian business history quietly broke up. It would be another 14 months before the major players would gather to officially ratify details of this incredibly complex and unusual deal in which private and public sectors would share both risk and reward. By then, the original agreement in principle had mushroomed to four fat volumes of terms and conditions.

ARCO PULLS OUT

THE SUDDEN WITHDRAWAL of Atlantic Richfield Co. (ARCO) from the four partner joint venture left a gaping hole in project financing — as well as some delicate matters of protocol to be addressed.

How did one say goodbye to a partner who had just sent the corporate equivalent of a "Dear John" letter?

How did one welcome three new government partners, viewed by many as "strange bedfellows" for the private sector to snuggle up with?

As Syncrude legal counsel in the 70 s, Jack Bjornson was in on both the hello and goodbye. "You had to wonder at the contrast. Gulf hosted a dinner for ARCO — one of those port and cigar events in a posh Toronto hotel with lots of flowers, white-jacketed waiters and gourmet food. It was truly elegant.

"The next meeting was with the three new government participants. We met in Esso's boardroom. They took us down for lunch, walked us through the cafeteria into the most spartan room imaginable with plastic tables and chrome chairs. Then they served us cold hamburgers and warm ice cream.

"It was obvious the owners were being gentle with ARCO because the company was experiencing a real cash crunch over the Alaska Pipeline. At the same time, the existing owners were showing the new owners how careful they were in running the operation."

As Gulf's McAfee told his shareholders following the Winnipeg Meeting, the unique government/industry pact represented "a landmark arrangement (that) may well set a pattern for meeting the enormous challenges posed by such ... projects as this, not only in Canada but also in the U.S. and elsewhere."

The media, held at bay until a final agreement was reached, now beamed the story across the country. Canada's biggest megaproject was back on track. In Edmonton and Fort McMurray, the news sparked emotional celebrations among both Syncrude and Bechtel people. Shutdown plans (prepared during the agonizing months of uncertainty) were hastily scrapped; and the word went out to factories around the world to push ahead on Syncrude contracts.

Syncrude Project Manager Chuck Collyer later summed up: "It was a great relief. But if you had seen how hard the owners fought to keep it alive, you would have had to believe in the final outcome. They were so determined, it encouraged all of us to try to maintain the credibility and integrity of the project while we waited for the final decision. Happily it was the right decision."

"SHORTLY AFTER THE WINNIPEG AGREEMENT, SENIOR EXECUTIVES FROM THE OWNER COMPANIES CAME INTO EDMONTON, LAID MONEY ON THE TABLE AND SAID, 'HAVE A PARTY!' WE DID JUST THAT — AT THE MAYFIELD INN. AS I RECALL, EVEN THE DRINKS WERE FREE. THE FEELING WAS A MIXTURE OF EXHILARATION AND RELIEF. SOMEHOW WE ALL FELT THAT WITH THE GOVERNMENTS NOW ON OUR SIDE, THE PROJECT WAS FINALLY ON FIRM GROUND."

GORD LORENZ, RESEARCH

A collective sigh of relief resounded through the province when the governments signed what became known as the "Winnipeg Agreement".

Soon, the furious pace of construction created an atmosphere charged with electricity and a near manic

A pressure vessel being transported to site for use in upgrading.

Opposite page: Bucketwheels move the oil sands onto the conveyor belt.

energy. The hefty injection of a rich tonic of secure financial backing fueled the project once again.

More trouble however, was hovering on the horizon. The project was suffering from high worker turnover and environmental groups were continually questioning the impact of the operation. Through it all, company employees tried to keep one step ahead of the incredible demands of the construction schedule while dealing with a multitude of human relations issues.

During its construction, Syncrude was rapidly gaining an international flavor and reputation. Reactor vessels were manufactured in Italy, pressure vessels were fabricated in France. Sweden produced centrifuges, Germany assembled bucketwheels and England created two mammoth furnaces for the megaproject. Syncrude also purchased its first computer, and inadvertently set another precedent …this time a legal one.

Three overly enthusiastic young computer "hackers" at the University of Alberta clearly had a sense of misplaced purpose, and no doubt brought

---

Below: Construction of a giant furnace used in the production of hydrogen.

grief to their families, when they used their considerable programming skills to gain access to the university's computer system. After determining Syncrude's password, they methodically replaced the company's account with an obscenity not generally found in most English language dictionaries.

While the young culprits were unquestionably pleased with themselves, the management of Syncrude, their parents, and the police were not amused. If the students' aim was to earn a place in history, they succeeded. As a result of their efforts, the Canadian Justice System defined the word "computer", in order to deal with the charge of "computer tampering".

"AFTER THE WINNIPEG MEETING, THERE WAS A MUCH BETTER UNDERSTANDING OF
THE PROJECT BY ALL THE PARTIES INVOLVED. THAT DOESN'T MEAN THAT ALL OF THE
GOVERNMENT/INDUSTRY PARTNERS SUDDENLY FELL IN LOVE WITH EACH OTHER —
BUT WE ENDED UP WITH A BETTER APPRECIATION OF HOW YOU HAD TO DO THINGS IN
THE DIFFERENT SECTORS. I THINK THAT HAS HELPED MAINTAIN AND SAVE THE PROJECT
MANY TIMES SINCE THEN. WE COULD SEE THAT THE PETROLEUM COMPANIES
INVOLVED COULDN'T POSSIBLY DO A SYNCRUDE BASED PURELY ON ECONOMICS.
THEY DID IT BECAUSE THEY REALLY FELT THE NEW LIFEBLOOD OF THE PETROLEUM
BUSINESS, IN CANADA IF NOT NORTH AMERICA, HAD TO BE THE TAR SANDS."

TOM VANT, CHAIRMAN, SYNCRUDE BOARD OF DIRECTORS,
AND CHAIRMAN, ALBERTA OIL SANDS EQUITY

Below inset: Pelly the Pelican, while making an unexpected pit stop at Syncrude in 1985, became covered in oil. After transportation by plane to the Brooks, Alberta wildlife centre he was soon cleaned up and ready to rejoin his feathered flock.

Right: Don Thompson, corporate secretary.

Below: Lower Camp, the Loon pond, 11 years after the pilot plant was shut down.

Left and below: Seedlings planted at Syncrude are part of the land reclamation process.

D on Thompson couldn't believe his eyes when he joined Syncrude as environmental coordinator in August 1979. "Here was a company with a full-fledged environmental program, something very unusual in industry at that time."

What he was witnessing was the continuation of an aggressive environmental research effort begun in 1969. At that time the company had begun probing the ecology of the area it was about to mine, meticulously recording information on fish populations, vegetation, and wildlife species ranging from mice to moose.

(Studies more than a decade later showed the area's wildlife to be remarkably philosophical about all the man-made activity. Far from vacating the area, many species had actually increased in numbers.)

Aurel Langevin, field ecologist assigned to the site in 1974, worked with construc-

tion forces to ensure everything from tree clearing to drainage activities was done in an environmentally acceptable way.

"Crews were clearing for the mine and there were these sandhill cranes nesting at the south end of the mining area. We waited until they left before we cleared there. It wasn't that they were an endangered species — but they were part of the natural environment and we weren't about to disturb them."

President Brent Scott later

reminisced, "We worked like dogs to make the plant environmentally acceptable, ensuring there was zero outfall to the Athabasca River and putting in all the Los Angeles-type pollution control equipment and remote sensing devices. It took a lot of effort but it paid off in the long run in terms of community acceptance."

THE GREENING OF SYNCRUDE

LONG BEFORE THE CATCH PHRASE "Think Green" became a part of the language, Syncrude was keeping on its environmental toes, always careful to promote a balance between the needs of man and nature. In 1972, the first of many environmental researchers joined the company. Dr. Ron Goforth, former research and environmental affairs manager said: "... the human use of the environment need not be destructive. With careful planning, based on good information, man-altered and natural ecosystems can exist in harmony."

Syncrude helped demonstrate that man-altered and natural ecosystems could exist in harmony.

Autumn scene along the banks of the Athabasca River.

SAVE OUR ENVIRONMENT

ENVIRONMENTAL GROUPS, reinforced by the media and provincial government, demanded assurances from Syncrude the environment would be protected. Of particular concern to the environmentalists was the emission of sulphur dioxide into the atmosphere. Save Tomorrow Oppose Pollution (STOP) suggested that a "killer fog" with harmful concentrations of sulphur dioxide would develop during the extremely low temperatures that often produce ice fog.

Syncrude asked a company from Calgary to prepare a report on this possibility. The report stated that the Syncrude plant would cause visibility problems at Mildred Lake in extremely cold temperatures, but the ice fog would not contain high levels of harmful pollutants.

To address these and other concerns, Syncrude hired five top scientists in the environmental field and helped establish the Alberta Oil Sands Environmental Research Program.

In response to criticism from the media, John Barr, then manager of public affairs, explained: "... the issue is not whether you can avoid environmental impact in oil sands development. You are always going to have impact. The issue is... can you impact on the environment in an intelligent, planned kind of way."

One example of Syncrude's determination to protect the environment and wildlife found in the area was the development of a small army of "Bitu-Men." These 23 mechanical scarecrows, with movable arms and noise-makers that sound like shotgun blasts, are used to keep birds away from the slippery temptations of the tailings pond.

As part of its commitment to return mined areas to their natural state, Syncrude has also established greenhouses which produce thousands of seedlings for reclamation each year.

Seedlings are grown in greenhouses for transplantation to reclaimed areas of the site.

These large 'bitu-men' are used to keep waterfowl away from the tailings pond. A propane cannon blasts at regular intervals to assist in the task.

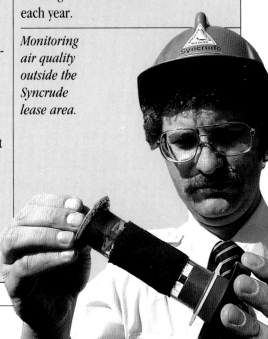

Monitoring air quality outside the Syncrude lease area.

D espite a staggering variety of delivery and logistical problems, construction was 50 per cent complete by the end of 1976. The first two draglines, 6,500 ton giants that mine the oil sands, were hauled to the site in pieces for assembly. At times, it must have looked like hordes of players trying to make the pieces of a mechanical jigsaw puzzle fit together.

Although the systems required to construct the plant were complex, the strategies required to house and feed more than 7,000 people were often mind-boggling. At least twice each week, trucks loaded with 600,000 pounds of provisions rumbled down the sometimes impassable road to deliver groceries to the camp. Every day, a staff of 380 prepared six hearty and wholesome meals to keep the workers happy and on the job.

Imagine if you can, cooking more than 11,000 pounds of meat, frying 19,000 eggs, peeling 4,500 pounds of fresh vegetables, washing 2,800 pounds of fresh fruit, brewing 480 pounds of coffee and pouring 2,700 quarts of milk daily!

I n the midst of construction, Syncrude also became the subject of a great deal of not always welcome attention from external, and often unexpected sources.

Larry Pratt, a University of Alberta political scientist wrote, "The Tar Sands", a less than complimentary book about the negotiations which had gone on between the oil companies and the provincial government during the licensing struggle.

A television program, described as "an explosive political drama zeroing in on power-brokering by the international petroleum industry" also captured the imagination of viewers and the attention of many.

While Frank Spragins was amused to find his name misspelled and pronounced incorrectly in the television show, then Premier Peter Lougheed did not find his portrayal a laughing matter. He launched a $2.75 million lawsuit against the offending station for defamation of character.

The intensity of the coverage and the desire to be first

The turntable of bucketwheel #2 is being lowered into place in May, 1977.

with stories on the project also led to occasional differences with the fourth estate.

One of the country's leading environmentalists, almost ran afoul of Syncrude safety regulations when he tried to enter the site sporting a beard. The rules require that people in all operations areas except the mine, be clean-shaven in order to be able to use Scott Air Paks, if required in an emergency. While his clean-

Malcolm Martin

shaven film crew shot segments for a television program a wistful spectre cooled his heels (and no doubt stroked his beard!) outside the plant's gates.

At one point in Syncrude's operational history, a Walt Disney film crew visited the site to collect footage for the new Epcot Centre in Florida. One of the centre's pavilions, dedicated to alternate energy sources, pictorially captures

A contractor working at Syncrude.

the history of energy. It spans from the age of dinosaurs through to today's larger-than-life mining machinery — all captured, in amazing "sensurround".

SETTING UP A NATIVE DEVELOPMENT PROGRAM

AT THE URGING of Frank Spragins, who made a long term commitment to create a native development program, a number of native advisers, including Alex Gordon, Terry

Right: Chief Ernest R. Houle of the Whitefish Lake Band.

Garven and Jim Carbery, then the assistant superintendent of schools in Fort Chipewyan, carved out the Indian Employment Opportunities Agreement. This agreement established one of the most successful native employment programs in Canada.

This agreement has since been replaced with another first – an agreement between the Athabasca Native Development Corporation, Syncrude and the governments of Alberta and Canada. All four groups pledge to work cooperatively to improve employment and business opportunities for aboriginal peoples in northeastern Alberta.

Cross-cultural training, aimed at creating a better understanding of the values of native

people as well as the expectations and needs of an industrial society, was integral to the program's overall success.

Although the company was initially plagued with problems of high turnover, Syncrude and the native leaders worked together to sort them out. Today, Syncrude is one of the largest native employers in the country

Jim Carbery, native development adviser, became an honorary chieftain for his work with the Cree and Chipewyan bands.

Left: Wilfred Ratfat, dragline operator.

Below: Peter Ladoucer, oil containment and recovery crew.

with over 300 full-time native employees. An additional 200 natives are employed through contract work.

As a tribute not only to Syncrude, but to Jim Carbery (who joined the company in 1979 as a native employment adviser), the Cree and Chipewyan bands in Fort Chipewyan made him honorary chieftain "Dene Kawechehat" (Cree for "He who helps") in 1985.

THERE'S NO PLACE
LIKE FORT McMURRAY

4

"THE FIRST TIME I EVER VISITED FORT
MCMURRAY, I WAS IMPRESSED BY THE SITE...
IT CAPTURED MY HEART. BUT, WHEN WE
CAME BACK INTO TOWN AND STARTED
LOOKING AT HOUSING, I TOOK A GOOD,
HARD LOOK AROUND AND SAID TO MYSELF
'WELL, IT CAN'T GET ANY WORSE'!"

JUNE THOMSON, (WIFE OF OGILVIE THOMSON)

"IN THE EARLY CONSTRUCTION
DAYS, I WORKED IN PAYROLL
AND ON MORE THAN ONE
FRIDAY EVENING, I HAD TO GO
INTO TOWN AND STAND IN
FRONT OF THE PETER POND
HOTEL, HANDING OUT
CHEQUES TO PEOPLE NO
LONGER LIVING IN CAMP."

SHERRY (BELL) PARSONS,
CENTRAL MAINTENANCE

THEY CAME, THEY SAW, THEY MADE MONEY

JUST AS THE OIL SANDS attracted some of the most talented, innovative and creative people in the world, it also drew more than its fair share of unsavory characters, out to make a substantive (though not necessarily honest) living.

The isolation of the North and the transient nature of the population provided a safe haven, at least for a while, for those evading the law. Card sharks, aware of the big dollars being earned by construction workers, made their presence felt. Rumor has it one shifty-eyed predator walked away with a grand total of $50,000 after a single game.

And a trailer from the southwestern United States, rumored to house several "ladies of the night", became a near legend in its own time. On a regular basis, this "loveshack" made frequent visits to a location just outside the camp gates for a stay of two or three days. (It is important to note, this is only a rumor. No one has indicated they ever actually visited the trailer; therefore a definitive identification of the occupants or their guests is impossible.)

A long with all this external attention came growing pains. When Great Canadian Oil Sands, which later became Suncor, began construction of its plant, the population of Fort McMurray began to spiral and the demand for essential services intensified. Until then, the tiny community of slightly more than 1,000 people was not

Housing in the Abasand area of Fort McMurray.

quite a part of the modern mainstream.

Almost without warning, however, the community was deflected forever from its peaceful, placid course. A huge influx of people came from throughout the province, country and indeed the world, to make Fort McMurray their home. They brought spouses, children, pets and a host of

medical, social, educational and recreational needs that had to be met. Houses, health care services, utilities, entertainment, recreational facilities, hair salons, dentists, banks and shoe stores were suddenly in great demand.

However, that was only the beginning. A decade later, when Syncrude appeared on the scene, residents of the new town of Fort McMurray shook their heads in consternation as the population increased faster than rush hour traffic on the way home from the plants.

The scramble to provide essential services was on again.

Northward Developments Ltd., Syncrude's housing affiliate and the largest developer in North America at the time, announced plans to invest nearly $200 million in new home construction to lodge 10,000 people in 2,700 homes and 1,500 rental units.

rink, so their kids could play hockey. "We got the land from parks and recreation, the boards were donated by a local lumber company, and we had the rink up and the ice surface ready by the end of the day."

M any outsiders described Fort McMurray as a "northern bush town, frozen solid as the tundra in winter and mired in muskeg the rest of the year." Former Mayor Chuck Knight, who worked for Royalite Oil for many years before answering the call of local politics, remembers the town more positively: "There was speedy development of shopping centres, movie houses, theatre facilities and virtually

One of the many housing complexes built by Northward Development to accommodate the population increase in Fort McMurray.

every type of recreational facility one can imagine. But the real growth came with the housing developments for Syncrude and Suncor. House values were literally going up over night. The real challenge was for us (the local council) to meet the demands for water, electricity and all those other services, related to

creature comforts, like paved streets and lights."

Although the town of Fort McMurray provided essential services such as utilities and roads; and, entrepreneurs delivered fanciful extras; the new residents, strangers from across the country and around the world, came together and built the "real" community that exists today. Ogilvie Thomson remembers one weekend, in the midst of a bitter cold spell, when a group of volunteers, mostly parents, spent the day building an ice

"THERE WAS ONE FELLOW FROM THE EAST, KIND OF A SPACED-OUT HIPPIE. I WAS NEVER SURE IF HE COULDN'T FIND A PLACE TO LIVE, OR IF HE DECIDED HE SIMPLY DIDN'T WANT TO BE TIED DOWN TO MATERIAL THINGS. ANYWAY, HE AND HIS WIFE GOT THIS HUGE OLD PACKING CRATE, FIXED UP THE INSIDE AND WERE LIVING THERE, WHICH WAS OKAY FOR THE SUMMER I GUESS... I WORRIED ABOUT WHAT THEY WOULD DO WHEN THE WEATHER TURNED COLD.

"WELL, THEY GOT SOME INSULATION AND THEY WENT OUT AND BOUGHT A LITTLE STOVE AND A LOCK FOR THE MAKESHIFT DOOR.

LO AND BEHOLD, SOMEBODY MUST HAVE SEEN SOME VALUE IN WHAT THEY HAD. THE FIRST DAY HE LEFT THE PLACE, AFTER HE GOT THE STOVE, SOMEONE BROKE IN AND STOLE THE THING!"

ED GORDON, RETIRED MATERIAL CONTROL

Getting stuck in the mud has been part of life in the mine.

"WATER, WATER EVERYWHERE..."

IN FORT MCMURRAY during construction, water was always an issue. There was either too little, too much, or what was available couldn't be used. Sherry (Bell) Parsons found the water in her then spanking new Silin Forest apartment sporadic at best, nonexistent at worst. "There were four renters, one on each corner, only two had water, and most of the time, I wasn't one of them." Not easily defeated, Sherry struck a deal with one of her neighbors; every couple of days, she'd pack her bathrobe, slippers, soap and such, and go to the neighbor's for a long, luxurious soak. Squeaky clean and content, with flashlight in hand, Sherry would toddle home along wooden planks that served as sidewalks, hoping she wouldn't lose her footing and fall in the mud, or worse yet, run into a bear.

"I don't think I was as worried about being attacked by a bear as I was by what I'd do if I fell into the mud before my next bath night!" explains the pragmatic Mrs. Parsons.

Driving on Highway 63 could be heaven or hell depending on which way you were going and the accompanying weather conditions. While the road normally looked like the Indy 500 or New York's 5th Avenue in rush hour traffic, a heavy rainfall could turn the 32 mile trek from site to town into a six hour sojourn through heavy sludge. When the skies turned gray and stormy, seasoned employees brought food, playing cards, reading materials and even sewing to keep them occupied while they waited to be hauled out of the goo.

* * * *

One winter, a few days before Christmas, a ruptured water main sent more than 20 families scrambling for dry land as more than five feet of water poured into their homes. Thanks to the near heroic efforts of Northward maintenance staff, the families were all nestled snugly in their own little beds in time for Santa's annual visit.

Stuck in the mud: Highway 63 as it was prior to paving.

Right: Brent Scott, second President of Syncrude Canada Ltd.

April 1977 will long be remembered for the flood that covered parts of the lower townsite.

IT NEVER RAINS BUT IT POURS

JUST AS SYNCRUDE was beginning to feel swamped with housing requests from the new recruits, Mother Nature dealt a bitter blow to the town in April 1977.

Floodwaters from the community's four nearby rivers rose 20 feet and flooded half the town. As a result, 1,500 people were briefly left homeless and cleanup costs reached a staggering $4.6 million.

While the abundance or shortage of water in Alberta's expansive north often tested the humor and tempers of residents, some demonstrated the ability to rise to the occasion. A trailer in the Park Plaza court sported a sign which proclaimed "As the tide came up, the beer went down." As silent testimony to this announcement, the sign was anchored with some 60 cases of (presumably) empty beer bottles!

BRENT SCOTT

A LARGE BLACK smudge on the map of Alberta in his public school geography book supplied youthful Calgarian Brent Scott with his introduction to the oil sands.

"I'm not sure I was too clear about the details but I certainly knew there was a lot of something up there." At that point he could hardly have imagined how the "something" would dominate his life. For close to a decade during the 1970s and early '80s, Scott would be the key figure facing the double challenge of building a plant and building an organization.

A civil engineer and senior executive with Gulf Canada, Scott joined Syncrude in 1972 as vice president and general manager. He was named president in 1975 when Frank Spragins became chairman of the Syncrude board of directors.

Cast in the same mold as his predecessor, Scott continued the Spragins' style of gentlemanly, open-door management. Although his early experience had been in projects (with Gulf he managed the singular feat of building two major refinery projects simultaneously), Scott quickly adapted to the business aspects and political sensibilities of his new post.

Described by former colleagues as "a superb manager of people," Scott placed a distinctive stamp on Syncrude's corporate culture that company veterans say remains intact today.

One longtime Syncrude observer notes that the emphasis on team management, and open communication that continues to dominate Syncrude life, is directly traceable to ideas and programs Scott introduced and supported.

Scott (now in Vancouver with his wife Lil following a stint in the United Kingdom with the Bechtel organization) looks back with particular satisfaction on the process of building the organization — from the busy recruiting campaigns he led in the 1970s to early efforts at unraveling the mysteries of team concept.

"When you think about staffing, it's quite remarkable. Without really screening for union bias, we were able to assemble 4,500 people who quickly learned to work very well in a team-concept environment."

He recalls that Syncrude owners withheld judgment on the experiment in team management. "They regarded it with a certain level of bemusement. Nonetheless it produced a project of good quality, on schedule, and as close as could be expected within budget. Later on, it helped to fashion the kind of organization the Japanese get so much credit for today."

- 325,000 cubic yards of concrete. This would be enough concrete to build 10 Edmonton Commonwealth Stadiums; the maze of structural steel used on the project could support 100 stadiums.
- the muskeg and earth moved for construction, piled layer for layer, would create another Great Pyramid.
- the pipes in the Syncrude plant would stretch from Fort McMurray to Calgary and half way back again.
- Syncrude's power plant could provide enough electricity for a city of 300,000 people; the wire and cable used in the plant could stretch from Fort McMurray to Toronto.
- During peak construction, there were no less than 10,300 people involved in building Syncrude.

W hen asked to describe Syncrude, even the most articulate individuals were often hard-pressed to come up with definitive adjectives to describe its magnitude. Words like "enormous", "gigantic", "colossal" and "humongous" were close but somehow failed to capture the project's scope.

It quickly became apparent Webster's Dictionary might have to come up with a new word to describe the project; particularly when one considers the volume of materials that went into (or out of) construction, including:

Above left and top right: Overburden (the top layer of sand, gravel and muskeg), is removed to reach the oil sand using large electric shovels.

Right: A comparison of the original control panel (inset) and the newer computer control system which replaced it in the early 1980s.

This display was part of the Syncrude campaign to recruit new employees.

THE GOLDEN HORSESHOE

Paul Hrabec of human resources was involved with the interviewing of nearly 8,000 applicants.

SYNCRUDE MANAGEMENT called it the Golden Horseshoe Campaign. Ontario probably viewed it as the Attack of the Eager Albertans – as Syncrude recruiters desperately searched for new workers.

A two week recruiting blitz in late 1976 took Syncrude President Brent Scott and an entourage of 25 recruiters to 10 major Ontario centres. Their goal: to let Central Canada know about the employment opportunities at Syncrude; and, if possible, snare the bulk of an estimated 2,000 people needed to operate the plant.

Earlier searches had concentrated on engineering and construction recruitment. Now the push was on for people to operate mining equipment, ride herd on complex extraction, froth treatment and upgrading facilities, and fill a clutch of administrative, clerical, and maintenance slots.

Start up was almost two years away but recruiters still remember the sense of urgency. Paul Hrabec of human resources was part of the action.

"We had 10 recruiting teams in the field, interviewing close to 8,000 applicants. This was after the federal Department of Employment and Immigration had screened out thousands of applications. In the end, job offers were made to nearly 1,200 applicants."

The success of the Golden Horseshoe Campaign sparked many similar efforts across the country. A year or so later, at an information session for potential employees, Syncrude recruiters were extolling the virtues of life in Fort McMurray, when the town suddenly made the national news in dramatic fashion. Media reports revealed that a major flood in Fort McMurray had produced horrendous evacuation problems.

"We had to do some fast pedaling — or was it paddling — to make sure we didn't sink and lose everyone in the audience."

Later campaigns would take the recruiters overseas — to Holland and Australia, England, Scotland and Wales. A booming economy and high employment levels at home pushed the search further and further afield.

At the height of hiring fever, Neil Lund, vice president and general manager, operations, observed it was easier to get people from the United Kingdom to pull up roots and cross an ocean than it was to entice southern Albertans to move north.

"Southern Albertans see Fort McMurray as nowhere. To somebody from the United Kingdom, all of Alberta is nowhere... north or south makes no difference."

JOB INTERVIEWS WAIT HERE

How many employees does it take to fill a dragline bucket?

By the end of 1976, construction was 50 percent complete, with assembly underway on the first two of the four huge 6,500-ton draglines which would be used to mine the oil sand. The machines had to be transported in pieces from across the continent and assembled at the Mildred Lake site. More than 80 operations people had cleared their offices out of Petroleum Plaza and the Financial Building in Edmonton. They formed the first wave of people permanently relocated to Fort McMurray.

"We now face the balance of the construction period with confidence, despite delivery and logistical problems," said Syncrude President Brent Scott as construction was halfway completed in 1976. "With start up only a year and a half away, enthusiasm is building. What was once very far in the future is now imminent."

On May 11, 1977, a representative from the Marion Power Shovel Company, climbed into the operator's seat of dragline number one, sounded three blasts of the siren and lifted the 360 foot long boom to a 40 degree angle about 200 feet off the ground. Thunder-storms threatened to delay the lifting of the boom, but the event went off without a hitch.

Then, on Victoria Day, 1977, Canadian Bechtel Ltd. handed over the final dragline to Syncrude mining operations. The dragline was "walked" from the construction pad to the mine, where it began its year-round excavation of oil sand.

President Brent Scott wrote to employees in 1977. "Any organization which has to achieve the size we do, in the time we have to do it in, is bound to have growing pains. We're no exception. But, even as we grow, we can see the different departments beginning to mesh, to support each other. Individual effort and increasing teamwork are combining to create a sense of purpose and achievement which is rapidly gaining momentum. We all have a common goal, to see the Syncrude project in operation and highly successful."

In late 1977, Frank Spragins was heard to say "Many of the production areas have been cleaned up and painted and I finally realized that the project is ready to roll. It's all over but the shouting!"

And shouting there was (or at least some constrained cheering) on September 15, 1978 at Syncrude's official opening as more than 700 people honored Frank Spragins. He was the man whose single-mindedness and unwavering conviction made the oil sands project a reality; despite stonewalling, delays and deferments that would have deflated a lesser man.

In just five years, the fierce determination of everyone involved in construction gave substance to a dream — a technological miracle that was carved out of sand, rock and muskeg.

It was a time for celebration, and celebrate they did. Barbecues, baseball games, boat races and dances were held in both Fort McMurray and Edmonton.

Frank Spragins

Pierre Trudeau, Prime Minister of Canada and Stan McQuitty, general manager extraction, touring the extraction plant.

Below: Mechanics in the mine's heavy duty shop.

John Barr, Syncrude's first director of public affairs, holds a model of a giant drop of oil to commemorate the 100 millionth barrel of oil produced in July, 1982.

MEDIA WATCH

A DOZEN YEARS AFTER STARTUP, Syncrude is still occasionally front page news. But at times, in its flamboyant history, the company has stayed squarely in the media spotlight for months at a time.

Sometimes hailed as a stunning success (at start up or on the 10th anniversary of production, for example), this unique and controversial energy giant also generated more than its share of skeptical and critical press — particularly in the early days when it had yet to prove its technical and economic viability.

John Barr, director of public affairs during construction, start up and early production, rates media coverage of Syncrude at the time at about a five. "That's on a scale of one to 10 where one is hostile and unfair reporting and 10 is fair and balanced reporting.

"Because of our prominence, anybody who wanted to take a shot at us could get an instant hearing and instant coverage."

As the economic impact of the project began to be felt, coverage was generally more favorable and informed, he recalls.

"Still we got a drubbing over start up problems and environmental matters. Our engineers, who were experienced with start ups, expected the early problems but apparently the public had much higher hopes. They expected it to work like a Swiss watch from the start."

Eventually, Syncrude's performance and corporate efforts to publicize company successes began to pay off. "I think we finally convinced the public the plant was neither scandalously designed nor incompetently operated."

There were a few shaky moments on opening day, including a temperamental coker that literally "flipped its gasket", spewing just enough hot, heavy oil to cause a small fire. Although the coker was resurrected briefly during the ceremonies, its kickoff antics were a sneak preview of the challenges ahead.

As is often the case with new ventures, the first year was also riddled with operational problems and personnel and machines were often at odds. Mother Nature, tyrannical and erratic at the best of times, had a penchant for demonstrating and enforcing her will. The fickle finger of fate was never far from triggering or collapsing Syncrude's newborn pulse.

Later that year, an explosion and fire ripped through two production lines in upgrading, and a skittish coker once again called it quits. Despite the setbacks, the company still produced a convincing 25,000 barrels a day and Syncrude's owners had succeded in establishing an impressive roster of clients for synthetic crude oil.

The oil industry was still keeping an inquisitive, critical and sometimes questioning eye on Syncrude. However, encouraged by the overall success of the operation, Shell Canada submitted a multibillion dollar proposal to the Energy Resources Conservation Board to construct a 140,000 barrel a day operation. The Alsands consortium was then formed and preliminary approval to construct a third oil sands plant was granted.

The Alsands consortium test facility northeast of the Syncrude project. September 1980.

ABASAND OILS LIMITED
FORT McMURRAY, ALBERTA

Alfred von Hammerstein
PRODUCER OF PETROLEUM, ASHPALT, NATURAL GAS & SALT.

SYNCRUDE
CANADA LTD.

International Bitumen Company, Limited
Offices: — 410 - 411 WILLIAMSON BUILDING.

200 YEARS OF RESOURCE DEVELOPMENT

OFFICIAL BICENTENNIAL SOUVENIR COVER

TEAM CONCEPT

FOR MOST, it was a strange new idea. For some, it sounded like an invitation to anarchy. And for those from a highly structured union environment, it was almost too bizarre to contemplate.

It was called team concept — and in the view of President Brent Scott, charged with building a vigorous and forward-looking Syncrude organization virtually from scratch – it was the only way to go.

What does it mean?

Corporate Secretary Don Thompson offers this explanation: "Team concept means everybody in Syncrude is considered by the company to be unique. Each employee has a valuable role to play and is part of at least two teams – their work team and the large team consisting of the entire company.

"The way the team leaders help Syncrude work teams accomplish their objectives is to make sure that everybody's ideas are listened to, weighed and taken into consideration.

BEST OF BOTH WORLDS

SOME EMPLOYEES came to Syncrude purely by accident — and saw their lives change dramatically as a result. Ken Hayward of Fairview, Alberta and Leita Affleck of Petawawa, Ontario can attest to that.

In the late seventies, both came to visit children who worked at Syncrude. "I never intended to stay," says Ken. "But then I got a chance to work at Syncrude so I stayed on."

Leita, too, was impressed with Fort McMurray and soon found herself working at the plant site.

"Team 5 brought us together in September 1979," Ken recalls. "I operated small equipment as part of site wide services and Leita was a sign maker. It was love at first sight!"

Married in 1981, the Haywards continued to function as a team on and off the site. Now

Leita and Ken Hayward met at Syncrude and were later married.

retired to St. Albert, they agree their respective "visits" to Fort McMurray were the best moves they ever made.

"I cried when I had to leave," says Leita. "It was a beautiful place to work. We both loved our jobs and we found each other — and that made the whole thing perfect."

14

Dennis Love, general manager, mine production.

There has to be a decision maker, of course, to help centralize all of this input. But the premise is that out of all of this input comes a decision which is better than it would have been had the leader acted without gaining the team's input."

Has it worked? Today, some of the earliest critics of this innovative management philosophy have become its greatest boosters, convinced that team concept has been the lubricant that's kept the organization rolling over some of the roughest industrial terrain ever encountered.

Most employees agree that the team approach has given them a stronger sense of confidence and commitment, a greater sense of belonging.

Bob Konowalec of mine mobile maintenance is convinced it also helps make the operation profitable. "If a company is looking after people's needs, team concept works beautifully."

General Manager of Mining Dennis Love admits he "didn't have a clue" about team building when he joined the company.

"I came from a union background so it was completely new to me. But when I saw the concept in action, I was so impressed we ran all our mine employees through team skills workshops. It's particularly important in the mine where many people — on draglines, or in trucks, for example — tend to feel a real sense of isolation."

Love discovered native employees instinctively exhibited excellent team skills — although they weren't likely to think of their behavior in those terms.

"Their traditional social structure has brought them together in groups. A lot of things they do are the result of discussion — and we were able to learn from that. In the end, all of our folks learned these skills very well and in my view the corporation still benefits from that."

Native employees from Fort Chipewyan work in mining's overburden department.

Right: There's no "off season" at Syncrude.

Left: Virginia Medleylane and Jack Lane enjoying Fort McMurray's winter

which arrived at site in the dead of winter. "It was minus 45 degrees. These guys, who left temperatures of plus 80 degrees in Texas the day before, had brought all this equipment fueled by oil and designed for a Dallas climate. Of course the equipment froze up. But not to be outdone, one of the guys got a very long extension cord and his blow dryer and tried to get the fluids moving again."

An employee wearing protective clothing to guard against the cold.

COLD WEATHER BLUES

THE ANALOGIES and adjectives used to describe winter in Oil Sands Country are colorful to say the least. One crane operator, delighted by prospects of the greenhouse effect, described an Arctic interval as "colder than my mother-in-law's kiss".

The frigid months are hard on workers and play havoc with the equipment.

One of the most stressful cold weather problems, in the early days, involved frozen toilets. It happened during start up, when winter winds turned particularly mean and "biffies" had to be kept in operation with the help of electric heat tracing on the cold water supply line.

One Syncrude staffer remembers a particularly painful incident. "A shout was heard, the toilet door burst open, and the user came flying out tugging up his pants. It seems the electric thermostat on the heat tracing malfunctioned and the water got so hot it turned to steam. Nobody seems to remember if first aid was required."

Geologist Gerry Lobb still laughs as he recalls a Texas geophysical crew

Cold weather testing of different bearing lubricants is carried out at research.

Below: A large lump of frozen oil sand was dug up in the mine in February, 1978.

START UP

5

Vice President, Operations, Jim Carter.

The first full year of Syncrude's operation was characterized by start-up problems. The original mining plan had envisioned the use of draglines to mine both overburden and oil sand. In actual practice, it was discovered that in some areas of the mine, the overburden could not safely support the immense weight of the draglines. To solve this problem, the company's overburden removal fleet was established in 1979 amidst some controversy.

break career decision for me. There were people saying: 'The trucks are going to sink out there and they won't go and we'll have to shut them down 45 days of the year, due to rain'. It was obvious there was a lot of controversy over whether or not they would work. I had to have the attitude they would."

There were also difficult ground conditions in the mine to deal with. Draglines and bucketwheels were bogged down in mud and damaged by frozen lumps of oil sand. In upgrading, a mid-winter

NORTHERN EXPOSURE

IN 1981, the National Geographic produced a special report on energy. Included were several spectacular photographs of Syncrude and the oil sands and the following observation: "Immense tar sands deposits, holding an estimated trillion barrels of oil, lie in the Canadian province of Alberta. Two large facilities extract the oil. They, together with South Africa's coal converting Sasols, are the vanguard in the measured march toward synfuels."

How fast would the "measured march" proceed? Reporters diplomatically reserved judgment on that one, saying simply: "In an emerging industry with the almost limitless possibilities of synfuels, can anyone foretell the future?"

Jim Carter, now vice president, operations, explains: "I proposed 170-ton electric drive trucks for the mine but the oil sand industry had not had a good experience with these vehicles and there were a lot of questions whether or not it was the right way to go. It was really a make-or-

failure in a heat exchanger caused hydrogen gas to escape into the cooling water system. The pressure broke a pipe, spewing water over the area and turning the nearby tower into an ice palace.

"Even if all plant conditions were perfect, it would still take time for people to come to

Winter operations on the conveyor transfer end of a bucketwheel.

grips with a brand new operation twice the size of anything that had existed previously", says Laird Wilson, former vice-president and general manager of upgrading operations. "You can't expect 3,000 to 4,000 people to turn into a smoothly functioning team overnight."

The rest of the industry was watching the company closely. In fact, the whole world was watching Syncrude's progress. Even Prime Minister Pierre Trudeau paid Syncrude a visit in 1978, joking with reporters in his usual style.

With only one production line functioning and continuing problems with the cokers, Syncrude was not required to pay provincial royalty payments the first year. A shortage of bitumen and a constant struggle to replenish the stockpile of oil sands continued to slow down operations; however, the company still shipped 18 million barrels of oil in 1979.

Meanwhile, the costs of the Alsands project had increased by a hefty billion dollars, and GCOS merged with Sun Oil to become Suncor.

Also during this period, the Alberta Energy Company decided to purchase 20 per cent of Syncrude, for the tidy

due to mechanical problems. Soon after one coker was up and running, a fire in one of the gas-oil hydrotreaters slowed production again.

The governments of Alberta and Canada were dragging their heels, having reached an impasse in oil price negotiations. The federal government threatened to rescind its promise to pay Syncrude world prices and six months later acted on the threat. Alsands was unceremoniously dumped on the back-burner, delayed for at least a year, and as it turned out, likely forever.

The same intestinal fortitude that prevailed during the lengthy process of obtaining a license to develop the project, provided stability and direction. Plans to increase production through the installation of new processing units, larger pipes, compressors and other equipment, given the unwieldy name of

---

Below: A major part of the debottlenecking project occurred in the diluent recovery units (more commonly known as Plants 7-1 and 7-2).

"debottlenecking", were projected to take five years. But the economic uncertainties of 1982 became cold reality and the second stage of the debottlenecking program was shelved.

The Petroleum Gas Revenue Tax had a dramatic impact on oil sands profitability, so the company announced a $10 million cut from its 1981 budget.

Anyone who thought the company had more than paid its dues, however, had another thought coming.

In a few short weeks,

sum of $570 million. In short order, the company sold half its shares for $365 million to Petrofina Canada Ltd. and Hudson's Bay Oil and Gas Company Limited, and increased the consortium to nine owners.

As the decade of the seventies drifted onto the pages of history books, the early eighties were marked with both successes and a series of problems which continued to challenge the Syncrude operation.

Production was curtailed for five weeks in 1980 when both cokers were shut down

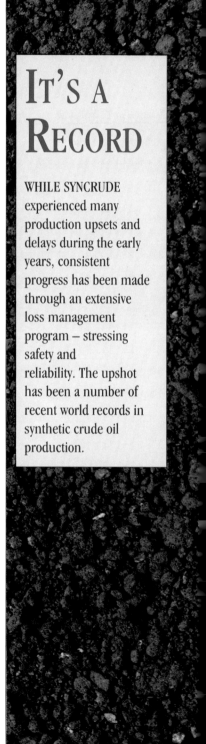

IT'S A RECORD

WHILE SYNCRUDE experienced many production upsets and delays during the early years, consistent progress has been made through an extensive loss management program – stressing safety and reliability. The upshot has been a number of recent world records in synthetic crude oil production.

stakeholders were dealt one stunning blow after another. But like agile cats with nine lives, they kept rebounding on their feet.

A fire temporarily disabled the tank farm.

Bucketwheel number one was taken out of service for six months when the diesel fuel used to lubricate the conveyor belts ignited, ravaging part of the machine.

A truck driver, dashing to the North Camp commissary to buy cigarettes, left his truck in neutral. The truck rolled into a natural gas line, rupturing it.

In a real stroke of misfortune, a worker trying to reignite a furnace pilot light in the commissary, triggered an explosion which injured 27 people.

A frozen air line caused a breakdown in both upgrading and utilities, resulting in nearly $3 million in lost production a day.

Just when everyone thought the worst was behind them, the temperature dropped to a brittle -35 degrees. Nature got much of the blame for the explosion and fire which devoured a hydrogen compressor unit in upgrading on

The rebuild of bucket-wheel no. 1.

December 20, 1980.

As a consequence, Syncrude's owners spent the holiday season shopping for companies willing to buy untreated crude oil.

There were no buyers. The company began to store the untreated crude and look at other alternatives. For once, luck was with them. The government gave the company permission to sell untreated naphtha outside Canada.

"THERE'S A THEORY THAT IF YOU FEED STUFF IN ONE END OF A PIPE, YOU SHOULD GET THE SAME AMOUNT OUT THE OTHER END. SO, IF YOU FIND YOU'RE NOT GETTING THE RIGHT AMOUNT, YOU'D BETTER DESIGN SOME CORRECTIONS AND FIX THE PIPE. THAT, IN A NUTSHELL, IS WHAT DEBOTTLENECK-ING IS ALL ABOUT. BUT INSTEAD OF A SINGLE PIPE, YOU COULD BE TALKING ABOUT A WHOLE PLANT.

"THIS IS WHAT WE DID IN 1983/84. IN SOME WAYS IT WAS EVEN MORE EXCITING THAN BUILDING THE ORIGINAL COMPLEX – BECAUSE YOU HAD TO DO THE WORK WITHOUT UPSETTING AN OPERATING PLANT. I REMEMBER ONE TIME A TRUCK DRIVER FORGOT TO LOWER HIS BUCKET AND CUT THE POWER LINE. INCIDENTS LIKE THAT CAN SHUT DOWN THE OPERATION AND THAT CAUSES A LOT OF STRESS. MANAGEMENT TENDS TO FROWN ON THAT SORT OF THING."

JOHN CULLITON, MINE DEVELOPMENT

THE WAY AHEAD: Production Records as of January 1, 1990

OVERBURDEN MOVED
(Mining)

YEAR
1989
53.37 million cubic metres moved.

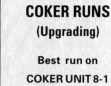

OIL SAND MINED BY DRAGLINES
(Mining)

MONTH
July, 1987
11.5 million tonnes of oil sand to extraction

YEAR
1989
110.36 million tonnes of oil sand to extraction.

BITUMEN PRODUCED
(Extraction)

WEEK
April 9, 1990
1.55 million barrels of bitumen produced

MONTH
October, 1989,
6.56 million barrels of bitumen produced

YEAR
1988
66.45 million barrels of bitumen produced.

COKER RUNS
(Upgrading)

Best run on
COKER UNIT 8-1
532 days between shutdowns
(46.6 million barrels of bitumen feed.)

Best run on
COKER UNIT 8-2
670 days between shutdowns
(59.4 million barrels of bitumen feed.)

SCO SHIPPED
(Upgrading)

DAY
November 13, 1988
214,100 barrels of synthetic crude oil (SCO) were shipped.

WEEK
April 30, 1989
1.477 million barrels of SCO were shipped

MONTH
May, 1989
5.73 million barrels of SCO were shipped

YEAR
1988
54.89 million barrels of SCO were shipped.

SAFETY

1989
Injury Frequency Rate
(medical aid and disabling injuries)
per 200,000 hours worked:
1.01.

Syncrude's third president, John Lynn relaxes in his new residence in Fort McMurray.

JOHN LYNN

JOHN LYNN recalls with characteristic humor and modesty his transition from construction manager to third president of Syncrude.

"In essence I was told, 'You built this thing, now it's up to you to see that the damn thing runs smoothly.'"

In fact, there was considerably more to the story. It began in 1974 when the youthful mechanical engineer, not long removed from his native Scotland and fresh from a major Imperial Oil refinery construction project in Sarnia, answered a call from former Imperial colleague Chuck Collyer.

As Syncrude's Project Manager, Collyer was on the lookout for an energetic and knowledgeable construction type to take on what many saw as a nearly impossible task — overseeing construction of Canada's largest energy megaproject.

Project observers would agree Lynn was the perfect choice for the job. Straight-talking, decisive and sociable, he commanded the respect of both construction crews and senior management.

As one colleague observed, "There's something about that Scottish accent, that pithy turn of phrase and that incredible candor. It makes you really believe in him. You find yourself wanting to do whatever he asks."

Lynn's own memories of the frenzied construction phase are tinged with a kind of giddy euphoria: "I don't think we were ever totally out of control but it seemed we were always skimming along on the verge. There were no 'experts'. We were doing new things and everybody was in the same boat. But somehow, between Syncrude and Bechtel, we managed to get this amazing, demanding project done."

Lynn clearly remembers driving south from Fort McMurray in 1978. Construction completed, he was moving into a Syncrude post in Edmonton and secretly thinking of moving on to another construction challenge, perhaps offshore.

It wasn't to be. The lure of the oil sands won and by 1979 he was back in Fort McMurray as vice-president of production. "I came as a professional

John Lynn with Prime Minister Joe Clark on tour in the mine.

project management guy and nobody was more surprised than I was when I learned how exciting and challenging operations could be. Team building, solving production problems — it was all great."

Named president in 1982, Lynn faced a new set of

challenges, including the start of a second massive capital investment program which consisted of phase one debottlenecking, plus CAP. This program would result in

John Lynn, participating in the Corporate Challenge, in Fort McMurray. Circa 1984.

another $1.6 billion being poured into the operation from 1983 to 1988, to boost production from 39 to over 50 million barrels of crude oil per year.

The first president to take up full-time residence in Fort McMurray, he and his wife Sylvia and their family happily immersed themselves in community life.

Today, as Project Executive of the OSLO Project, Lynn admits he sometimes experiences a sense of deja vu. "OSLO involves the next generation of technology and certainly it will have its own challenges and excitement. But I know nothing can ever match the exhilaration of the Syncrude experience."

Contractor training on Scott Air Pak equipment in Edmonton

A s early as 1978, Syncrude's concern with the safety and physical well-being of its employees was demonstrated. The company announced a major study of the effects of prolonged exposure to bitumen on workers. Based on a series of medical tests at the onset, workers would be monitored for 10 to 15 years.

Interim results indicate some minor concerns with skin problems and respiratory difficulties during shutdown periods and further research in these areas is being conducted.

The company also had a comprehensive, tried and

tested emergency response plan. The strong commitment to the personal safety and well-being of employees has dealt with both on and off the job issues.

However, despite near heroic efforts to stem

Practice runs keep the emergency response teams in prime condition.

accidents, a tragic event in early 1981 cost two contractors their lives. In response, the company took a hard-line position on ensuring similar accidents would be avoided by making it compulsory for all contract employees to take safety training before they were allowed on site.

Safety measures also took on a new dimension when intensive training programs aimed at preparing emergency response crews were put into place.

"THERE WERE A LOT OF NEAR MISSES AT SYNCRUDE DURING THE
1980s – INCIDENTS LIKE FIRES AND THE TIME THE CONTRACTOR KNOCKED
OUT AN ELECTRICAL DUCT BANK. WHAT SAVED THE DAY – AND LEFT US
FEELING POSITIVE ABOUT THE EIGHTIES – WAS THE WAY PEOPLE WORKED
TOGETHER TO GET BACK ON TRACK. I REMEMBER PEOPLE IN OUR AREA
DOING BOTH THEIR NORMAL WORK AND COLLECTING DATA FOR
INSURANCE CLAIMS. IT WAS THAT WAY ALL OVER THE SITE – PEOPLE
REALLY PULLING TOGETHER LIKE THEY DO IN TIMES OF DISASTER.
I THINK IT'S SOMETHING WE CAN ALL BE PROUD OF."

B. E. (BORIS) LITWIN, ROYALTIES ACCOUNTANT

Visits to Fort McMurray schools teach local school-children about safety.

I n March 1982, Brent Scott's commitment to employees' safety was underscored after two major incidents, attributed to human error, caused major work disruptions. He pointed out that people are the key to safety, and managers and supervisors have major responsibilities in that area. "... some managers don't realize you can't influence a machine. When people say you're too concerned about people, I say: 'what the hell else is there?'"

Left: Extensive fire fighting training takes place at the Lower Camp Fire School.

Below: Contractor in vessel entry protective clothing.

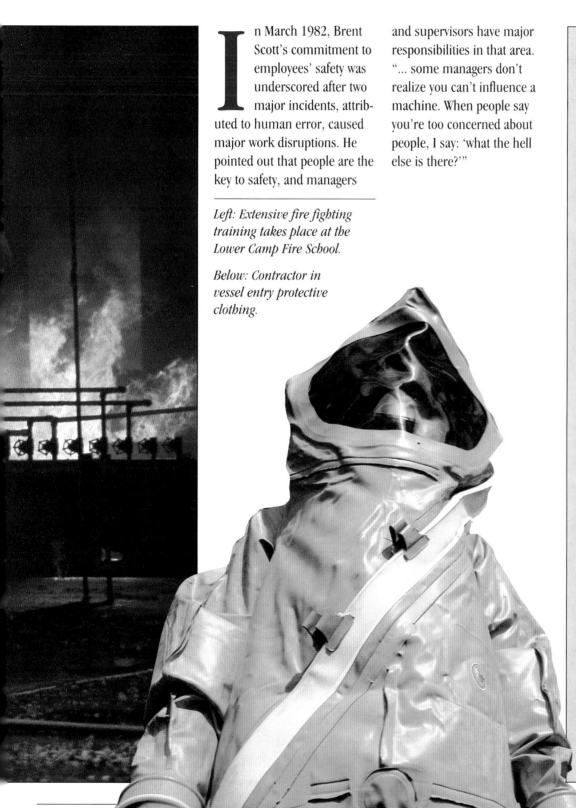

BATTLE OF THE SAFETY MASCOTS

SANDY THE Safetysaurus, long viewed as the Mohammed Ali of safety mascots, found his title threatened when a bright young upstart, Safety CID, entered the ring.

But the overconfident CID fell from grace with a bump, thud and a skid. A few astute, diehard fans of Sandy's took issue with CID's short sleeved shirt, a definite faux pas by Syncrude safety standards.

CID's trainers and manager did a little rethinking and a lot of redesigning before their champ went out again to try for the title.

But it quickly became clear that CID was only shadow boxing... Sandy the Safetysaurus had regained (at least for the moment) the upper hand!

"ONE CORNER OF THE EXTRACTION PROPERTY ALONG THE ROAD TO THE MINE WAS ALWAYS A MESS, A REAL MUD HOLE, AND I WAS ALWAYS AFTER THE MAINTENANCE PEOPLE TO CLEAN IT UP BECAUSE IT WAS SUCH AN EYESORE. AFTER I RETURNED FROM MY HOLIDAYS IN LATE SPRING OF 1980, I WALKED AROUND THE CORNER AND FOUND A PROMINENT SIGN THAT READ 'STANLEY'S PARK'. AUSTIN HOWARD, THE MAINTENANCE SUPERVISOR, HAD A BUNCH OF GUYS CLEAN UP THE AREA, FILL IT WITH TOP SOIL, PLANT TREES, PUT UP A FENCE AND RAISE A FLAG POLE. IT WAS LIKE A LOVELY OASIS IN A SEA OF CONCRETE AND STEEL."

STAN McQUITTY, (FORMER EXTRACTION, GENERAL MANAGER)

SYNCRUDE IN THE COURTS

Jack Bjornson

FOR ALL ITS HIGH PROFILE multi-billion dollar presence, Syncrude Canada Ltd. has been embroiled in surprisingly few lawsuits during its 25 year history.

Two major disputes with Bechtel, major contractor for the original plant, were settled out of court. According to Jack Bjornson, retired corporate legal counsel, many other potential court fights also fizzled in the face of "reason and accommodation."

Because of the massive size and specialized nature of the project, it was no secret that often only one company could do the work. "If the job didn't go perfectly, it was preferable to deal with the person whose work you knew rather than somebody new. Instead of turfing a guy out and suing him, we figured it was better to try and work with him."

Ray Hansen, Bjornson's successor as head of the legal department, notes Syncrude completed its 25th year with its courtroom record intact.

"We've never lost a case. One reason is we approach litigation like a business. Syncrude only undertakes litigation that we're convinced will be successful. We don't approach disputes with emotion. If we know we've done wrong, we make amends and don't get into excessive legal hassles over the matter."

Hansen is equally proud of the company's record in the human relations field. "Since 1985, only two letters of complaint against Syncrude have been submitted to the Human Rights Commission and both were satisfactorily resolved."

The early eighties were a disappointment to those in the industry who had played a part in launching the project. In the zealous seventies, every hurdle was nothing more than a nuisance, an obstacle to be dealt with, before moving on to bigger and better things.

The federal budget, the National Energy Program and the seemingly endless verbal battle between governments took a tremendous toll; not only on the oil industry but on the overall economy of the province. It was estimated that 8,000 jobs in the oil-field were lost, 72 oil rigs temporarily pulled out of Canada, and government policies became blockades to profitable operations.

On September 19, 1980, the Alsands consortium shelved its plans for development. Amoco also abandoned a $46 million "in-situ" pilot plant at Gregoire Lake.

Soon, a gray, crippling air of uncertainty gripped the oil industry. At Syncrude, the fear of a complete shutdown was tangible. The fragility of the giant was frightening. Tension and anxiety were prevalent: morale fell. The frustration of not knowing what the future held mounted; so did the pressure.

In May 1981, an illegal strike by employees of contractors working for Syncrude took place and 2,000 contract workers walked off the job. A week later, when it looked as if the troubled waters had been stilled, 50 workers were involved in a riot in the camp kitchen; one worker was assaulted and two bunk houses were set afire.

Bears feeding at the Syncrude landfill site in the early 80s.

Stanley's Park, named after the first General Manager of Extraction, Stan McQuitty.

Apart from regular safety concerns, there were specific concerns about the construction site's remote location. Workers were given courses in wilderness survival. But no course could have prepared one bus driver for the furry passenger he picked up.

An enterprising young bear, in search of an easy meal, boarded a bus where workers routinely left their lunch bags. The bear then proceeded to rummage through the contents of the lunch.

The bus driver boarded his bus and started to drive away, before he noticed in his rear view mirror, a rather large creature coming down the aisle. He didn't need a wilderness survival course to know he'd better stop and exit before his disgruntled passenger.

Bear and bird stories continue to play a significant role in the history of Syncrude's development. As people moved into wildlife's natural habitat, there were numerous encounters and major concessions made by all.

Perhaps the most famous story, which has now achieved near legendary notoriety, revolves around a black bear's untimely and unwelcome visit to the site's medical centre. The nurse on duty had some trouble convincing security that the midnight intruder was a large hairy creature walking on all fours.

Over the years, the big beasts were found in the operator's seat of a tractor, in camp kitchens, road ways, and recreational facilities.

In terms of our feathered friends: ravens, feather-bloated in winter to the size of cats and described as "ravenous black birds", have tried to eat their way through virtually everything and anything they could get their beaks on; including, and possibly for shock value, electrical cables.

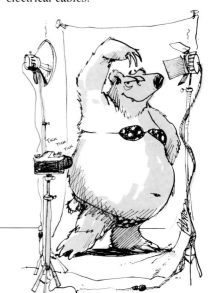

Left: Born June 14, 1981, Lisa Marie Ahyasou of Fort MacKay is the only baby to have been born at the Syncrude site — so far.

Below: Lisa at age seven.

A Star is Born

DESPITE THE hard times, there were some small blessings that involved a different kind of labour. One came in the form of tiny Lisa Marie Ahyasou, born with the help of nurses, in June 1981, at the medical centre on site. It seems Lisa, the youngest of four children, surprised everyone, especially her mother, when she decided to make an early appearance on the trip from Fort McKay to the hospital in Fort McMurray. A detour off the highway, and onto the site, gave nurses on duty the chance to hone their birthing skills.

To underscore the joy surrounding Lisa Marie's birth, the medical centre proudly touted a sign which read: "Syncrude Maternity Ward, No Appointment Necessary, Free Delivery Service, No Storks Past This Point!"

After nearly five years of operation, the man who was credited with masterminding the construction of the Syncrude site, resigned his position as president and chief executive officer.

Brent Scott said "What I came to do is pretty well done; I want to tackle a different challenge for the rest of my career." Before he left, Scott had to perform a most unpleasant task. Syncrude announced a hiring freeze and the need to reduce the 1982 operating budget by $70 million. Apprehension clouded the site. Words like "redeployment" and "redundant" peppered daily conversations. Job security became a major concern (though there were no layoffs); and the ambience of the work place became guarded.

Although President John Lynn, affectionately known as "the Scottish Connection", had barely settled into his new office in 1982, he was soon confronted with a number of major upheavals, ranging from labor disputes, equipment failure, lost production time, and fires to the realization that the Alsands project was in the midst of its swan song.

By May 1982, the Alsands consortium was dissolved; the city of Fort McMurray went into mourning and a sense of impending doom was evident.

Premier Peter Lougheed's response to the Alsand's demise was: "Perhaps it's the era of "small is beautiful." New Syncrude President John Lynn's response to the premier clearly indicated his disagreement. He said: "We have to wonder if they don't really mean small dreams and small accomplishments. It's not a pretty future if we listen to the prophets of doom and gloom. I believe megaprojects can be key ingredients to our economic future...in the Alberta oil sands, we have a tremendous resource that lends itself perfectly to megaprojects. Let's get on with it!"

This attitude was seconded by employees.

While job security was a concern in the early eighties, environmental issues were also coming to the forefront.

At Syncrude, the development of a new overburden disposal site was delayed when the Fort MacKay Band took exception to the process because it would disturb the trapline of a band member.

BRIAN PAPINEAU, MANAGER,
FINANCIAL SERVICES

Above: In 1982, the premier toured the Syncrude site to celebrate the 100th million barrel of oil.

A s usual, winter that year had a profound impact on both people and production. In an attempt to eliminate some equipment problems, the company embarked on an extensive winterizing program. One manager captured the essence of the project and the problems when he said: "The equipment is the best in the world... for a mild climate. (But) Syncrude is fighting a winter war with summer equipment."

The spring of 1984 brought the largest maintenance shutdown in the company's history. During this period the mine kept running and in a stroke of good fortune, an area that had previously been thought unmineable yielded enough oil sand to feed the enormous appetite of the plant for five months.

However, angry summer storms, dumped millions of gallons of water on the operation and caused draglines to come to a grinding halt. They also created power outages and made impassable roads an everyday occurrence.

Ironically, just when water was at its most abundant, the company launched a new energy and water conservation program, under the "Encon" banner. Within a year, the company had slashed $11 million off its utility bills.

The trapper in question regularly crossed Syncrude's lease and took photographs that put the company's waste disposal practices in question. Alberta Environment stepped in to investigate, the company was cleared, and eventually an amicable agreement was worked out whereby the trapper was compensated for the loss of a portion of his trapline and allowed to continue trapping on Syncrude property.

The summer of 1982 brought some welcome relief in the form of good news. Soon after the company produced its 100 millionth barrel of oil, it announced it would move forward with a three year, $180 million "debottlenecking" project, designed to increase the daily output of synthetic crude by 10,000 barrels to 119,000 barrels per day.

Above: Employee in the carpentry shop.

Left: Maintenance is crucial to the plants' operations.

DVX

BY THE TIME Syncrude moved its head office from Edmonton to Fort McMurray in 1983, the term "office automation" was already old hat in most business circles. Syncrude gave the concept a new twist, however, by installing a leading edge voice mail system called Digital Voice Exchange or DVX.

A marriage of computer and telephone technologies, the system involves the use of 1,700 computerized message centres or "mailboxes" snugly tucked away in the bowels of a powerful computer that forms the heart of the system.

"I couldn't begin to estimate the number of memos, meetings and phone calls DVX has saved," says Ray Beswick, project leader, management control/bureaucracy reduction program, who spearheaded installation of the site-wide message system.

WHAT MAY HAVE STARTED OUT AS AN ECONOMICAL MEASURE TO REDUCE THE COSTS ASSOCIATED WITH OPERATING VEHICLES ON SITE, TURNED OUT TO BE A FITNESS BOOM WHEN HORDES OF EMPLOYEES STARTED TO USE "PEDAL POWER" TO MAKE THEIR WAY AROUND THE SITE.

When Syncrude officials announced in the early 1980s they would soon be producing more than a barrel of synthetic crude from every barrel of bitumen processed, more than one observer understandably raised a skeptical brow.

The secret that would help the company pull off this bit of magic was the bitumen hydrocracker.

Installed as part of the $750 million Capacity Addition Project completed in 1988, the hydrocracker works in tandem with the plant's two existing fluid cokers to upgrade bitumen feedstock.

The wizardry that produces more than 100 per cent yield centres around the addition of hydrogen to bitumen in the hydrocracking process.

While this technical sleight of hand was being conducted by Capacity Addition Project engineers, elsewhere in the base plant, other production miracles were unfolding. Debottlenecking, technical innovation, and a determination on the part of everyone involved to "keep doing it better" were producing tangible results. As a result, today's production far exceeds even the most optimistic

Shelves of coveralls show only part of the clothing supplies available to Syncrude employees.

projections which were being made when CAP was being designed.

The Capacity Addition Project was to have added 6.8 million barrels annually to production, says Thane Waldie, vice president, technology. "By the time we had it completed similar gains had already been made in the base plant. This means we're looking at more than 13 million additional barrels a year — or close to 60 million barrels in 1990."

However, the wizardry doesn't stop there. Vice President, Human Resources Phil Lachambre points to yet another bit of Syncrude legend.

"When we started up the plant we had around 3,700 employees for a plant designed to produce approximately 40 million barrels a year. We expect to achieve this year's budgeted 60 million barrels — a 50 per cent increase — with just 4,600 employees. We're continually developing our people and the technology to do more and more with less and less."

FASHION FLAVORS

CLOTHING ALWAYS played an important role in overall operations.

Not since Eve turned a fig leaf into a fashion statement had the focus on appropriate dress taken on such significance. Hard hats, steel toe boots, protective overalls, eye guards and insulated gloves not only added to the safety of the operation, but often added to the comfort of the wearer.

Ultimately, "finding oneself" at Syncrude took on new meaning as employees and contractors also

Protective safety wear used by Syncrude employees.

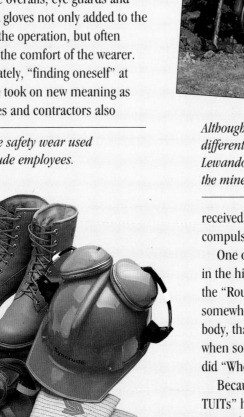

Although protective clothing may vary in different parts of the operation, Dennis Lewandoski displays the clothing used in the mine area.

received identification tags, now compulsory fashion accessories.

One of the most sought after treasures in the history of the company is related to the "Round TUITs", circular buttons worn somewhere on the upper portion of the body, that needed only to be pointed to when someone asked, as they inevitably did "When are you going to...?"

Because of their popularity, "Round TUITs" have become as rare as a dodo bird; rumor has it that they command a very high price from button and pin collectors!

GROWING PAINS 6

Maintenance workers inside an extraction tumbler.

The announcement of the multi-million dollar Capacity Addition Project (CAP) expansion brought renewed faith in spring, 1984. The project would create 400 new permanent positions and an additional 2,000 temporary jobs during the construction phase.

Close on the heels of the CAP announcement, the provincial government agreed to a change in tax structures involving special royalty breaks that would reduce the risk of failure for the oil sands projects.

The price of oil rose to $29 (US) per barrel and the future looked brighter than it had in some time.

Less than two months later, however, fate once again hammered the Syncrude operation. A fire followed by an explosion occurred on one of the cokers. Production of synthetic crude oil was suspended indefinitely as the company assessed the damage and made arrangements to have bitumen trucked to Suncor for processing.

Shutdown! Early in Syncrude's operating history, the word was most often associated with emergencies — the unsettling "crashdowns" that occurred when fire, explosion or any one of a dozen technical snarl-ups knocked out cokers, hydrotreaters or other vital links in the production train.

Such events crippled production for weeks at a time and called on all of the resources of Syncrude and outside contractors to get the

Tony Czarniecki, manager of construction for the Capacity Addition Project (CAP), shows a scale model of a CAP unit.

operation back on stream. (At a time when synthetic crude fetched $40 a barrel, such incidents were particularly painful).

As one longtime shutdown observer puts it, "When you see the plant losing millions of dollars everyday because of some totally unplanned, unanticipated foul-up in the system, you don't waste time — you

COKER TROUBLE

A DEVASTATING FIRE on one of the cokers in upgrading made for a hot August night in the summer of 1984. Amazingly, no one was injured in the fire; it occurred only hours after a shift change, otherwise the area could have been full of employees. A massive recovery program was instituted, but President John Lynn's first concern was to reassure shaken workers that the company would indeed continue with its operation.

The west wall of the compressor building shows more of the damage which occurred in the coker fire. This wall was opposite the most severely hit area.

Below: On August 15, 1984, a major fire occurred at coker 8-2. In this photo, the coker is totally hidden by the dense smoke.

Inset: The main pipe alley on the fire-ravaged coker shows some of the damage to the piping in the area.

Synergy was a popular communications vehicle during the early 80s.

While Syncrude spokesmen applaud today's improved operating and safety record, they admit they're proud of the way the company responded to past incidents.

For Tony Grace, then in shutdown maintenance and production, the company's 1984 success in quickly bringing a disastrously fire-damaged coker back on stream, stands out as a highlight of his 15 year career with the company.

"We were on vacation when we heard about the coker fire. It was the most serious incident we've ever had, in terms of dollar losses, but

Left: The air blower, on the coker, being reassembled during the major rebuild in 1984.

Vice President, Administration, Tony Grace.

just get to work on the problem and get it fixed as fast as you can."

Even when shutdowns were expected, there seemed at first to be an element of chaos attached to them, recalls Don McNeil, who took over responsibility for secondary upgrading shutdowns in 1981.

"Nobody knew exactly what to do in those early days. It wasn't that we lacked resources or expertise; it was just that the plant was so new

and different, nobody knew what to expect.

"The philosophy was: sound the bugles and the cavalry would come roaring over the hill. By tradition, you would need 100 pickup trucks, 1,000 men, and 100 per cent overtime!"

Gradually, increased operating experience, steady progress along the learning curve, ongoing engineering improvements and modifications and investments in

safety, housekeeping and maintenance, changed the picture.

Today, the scheduled shutdown has become the norm. And while incidents can still occur to upset the timing of these well-planned maintenance outages (as on December 15th, 1989, when a fire in a gas-oil hydrotreater cut production by one third for several weeks), the crisis mentality about shutdowns has largely disappeared.

Overburden is used to replace the oil sands in the mined areas.

miraculously no fatalities or serious injuries resulted.

Grace would soon learn that the rebuilding process amounted to a mini-version of the original project. "There was this fantastic spirit. Everyone wanted to get the job done and nothing was allowed to get in the way."

In the end, the company spent $100 million in 100 days

Secretary of Defense and persuaded him to lend us a couple of U.S. Air Force Galaxies."

Grace notes they were the only planes in the world big enough to do the job. "In just two flights they saved us weeks of time."

— but the coker was back in business well before the date anticipated by management.

"We just wouldn't take no for an answer. For example, when we needed some huge cargo planes to bring in needed equipment, the request went out through Secretary of State Joe Clark. He, in turn, talked to the U.S.

This photo shows the piperack after most of the rebuild was completed. Nearly all of the piping shown is new.

TOUGH WAY TO LEARN

ON THE WAY TO TODAY'S impressive safety and reliability records, Syncrude operating teams had plenty of opportunity to learn that what can go wrong, almost certainly will.

A case in point: the time in 1985 when utilities single-handedly shut down the whole plant. Mishap followed mishap in a spectacular domino effect that crippled production for 45 days.

John Dubeau of utilities remembers it this way: "It was a comedy of errors. An operator went out to test an instrument and that's when it started. The instrument was hooked into a system that caused it to trip. One of our other pieces of equipment was down for mainte-nance. Then its backup wouldn't start.

"We had almost 30 minutes to get something going. We lost our boilers. We lost our instrument air and then upgrading lost control of their instruments. Everybody was running around trying to put them on manual. Next we lost the cokers and in the meantime we were losing boiler steam. In short, everything went haywire.

"We were really caught with our pants down and the result was a 45-day outage of the whole plant. We dumped everything.

"If there was a positive side to the nightmare, it had to be this: It was a mighty effective one-time learning experience!"

Jim Carbery, native adviser with Syncrude, and Joe Dene in Fort Chipewyan.

On April 1, 1985, Ralph Shepherd, a senior vice president with Imperial Oil assumed the position of president and chief executive officer of Syncrude. John Lynn, the personable Syncrude construction pioneer, returned to Esso Petroleum as the senior executive in charge of the large oil refinery and lubricating oil complex in Sarnia, Ontario.

Initially, Shepherd seemed somewhat aloof and imposing. He also aroused the attention of the local media when he

Painting of Ralph Shepherd, Syncrude's fourth president, by upgrading employee Rudy Pongo.

took possession of a spectacular new home that became something of a showcase in Fort McMurray. Eventually, however, his quiet tenacity would triumphantly lead the

company through some very difficult times. It would also earn him the respect and admiration of not only employees, but the press as well.

That spring, discussions centred around a major expansion that would increase the company's production capacity by 50 per cent. In spite of an economy that could best be described as "collapsed", Syncrude forged ahead with its expansion studies. John Zaozirny, the Alberta Energy Minister, announced in March 1985, new oil sands plants and expansions to existing plants would not be taxed on their revenues. This, in addition to the phaseout of the Petroleum Gas Revenue Tax, gave the company a much needed financial shot in the arm.

REMOVING BARRIERS TO EMPLOYMENT

IN THE 1980s, Syncrude established new employment equity measures aimed at recruiting not only local employees, but providing equal employment opportunities to natives, women and people with disabilities. Notes Vice President, Human Resources Phil Lachambre: "We've made great progress in this area, with year over year increases in our workforce of natives and women in non-traditional roles."

Women are involved in all aspects of Syncrude's operations.

Tour guide Jackelene Fox has taken many visitors through the Syncrude site. She notes, "Visitors from other cultures are often fascinated at the way women are part of this company. It's second nature for us to have women working as truck drivers or engineers."

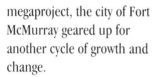

The company employs natives in a variety of capacities across the site.

Optimism and confidence in the oil sands were high in 1985. An Energy Resources Conservation Board report predicted that the oil sands would compensate for declining conventional oil supplies, providing two-thirds of the province's oil production soon after the turn of the century. There was talk of reviving the Alsands project and murmurs of the need for a third major facility in the province's north east quadrant. Never one to back away from an oil sands megaproject, the city of Fort McMurray geared up for another cycle of growth and change.

A month later, reality hit home once again. World oil prices began to plummet. Ralph Shepherd alerted management about potential budget cuts if the price continued its downward spiral; it did, and Shepherd acted quickly. In a concise memo to staff, he wrote: "Crude oil prices are decreasing which leaves no alternative but to reduce costs in order to maintain profits and cash flows."

The reaction, both at the plant and in the town, was similar to people listening to chalk scratch the surface of a blackboard. Hackles went up, enthusiasm went down. Nerves were on edge, confidence ebbed. Fortunately, employees rallied and soon ideas on cost savings and improvements were rolling in.

Interior and exterior views of the Oil Sands Interpretive Centre.

INTERPRETIVE CENTRE: OIL SANDS SHOWPIECE

"WE WERE literally watching oil sands history disappear through vandalism, deterioration and neglect," says Syncrude employee and long-time Friends of the Athabasca Oil Sands volunteer Bernie Steinraths.

"In the 1970s, there were several Syncrude employees who were concerned that important monuments to decades of oil sands activities were in danger of being lost forever.

"It was ironic because all of this was happening at a time when the rest of the world was getting fired up about oil sands and this area was receiving requests for information from all over the world. We obviously needed a place to preserve some of this equipment and history and act as a clearing house for oil sands information."

Luckily, there were people at Suncor and a number of teachers and other community residents who shared this interest.

Kenn Burgar, another Syncrude employee, headed up the group as chairman of the original advisory committee to the Ministry of Culture. Soon northeastern Alberta Regional Commissioner Vic Henning threw his enthusiastic support behind the idea. The group designed a building and tried unsuccessfully to get government funding.

Sometime later, the idea

caught the eye of then Premier Peter Lougheed and Burgar, Steinraths and company stood back and watched the action.

"Lougheed was a great booster of the oil sands. Once he got hold of the idea, it got on track immediately — like the next day. The whole thing was on the fast track and by 1985 the Oil Sands Interpretive Centre was a reality."

The early boosters were overwhelmed, says Steinraths. "We had envisioned more of a technology centre with some historical elements thrown in. This was slightly different — but we all agree Fort McMurray ended up with a first-class facility."

Now attracting up to 80,000 visitors a year, the centre is even more successful than its earliest supporters had hoped.

"It allows you to not only see and touch history — it also lets you imagine the future of the oil sands," says Steinraths.

RALPH SHEPHERD

IN APRIL 1985, when Ralph Shepherd accepted the position of Syncrude president, he did so with a couple of strong convictions. One was that it would be the most challenging and interesting job he had ever tackled. The other was that it would be the last in a long string of management posts he would fill during a close to four-decade career in the energy industry.

He says he was right on both counts. First, he did indeed find the Syncrude

assignment the most exciting and interesting he had ever tackled. Second, as planned, he and wife Marj have retired near Creemore, the Ontario town where he grew up.

That's not to say Shepherd experienced any lack of challenge throughout a career that began with Imperial Oil in 1951. A graduate in chemical engineering from the University of Toronto, he quickly

developed the management skills which would lead him from Sarnia to Regina, overseas to Exxon operations in Denmark and the Netherlands, then back to Sarnia and Toronto.

"I'm delighted I decided to accept the Syncrude appointment, even though during my time there the business environment was worse than anyone had ever anticipated."

While Shepherd expected crude oil prices would fall in

Marjorie and Ralph Shepherd

An employee meeting led by Ralph Shepherd in 1986.

the late 1980s, no one anticipated such a dramatic plunge. Balancing the shock, he recalls, was the unusual level of understanding and loyalty displayed by employees.

Faced with the unpleasant task of managing during a major industry downturn, he discovered to his delight that "everybody understood the economics of the operation very well. They knew the company was at risk in a monetary sense and I think that's why the response to Syncrude's cost-cutting efforts was so great."

Remembered best for the series of forums in which he faced employees to explain Syncrude's tough-times strategies, Shepherd is credited

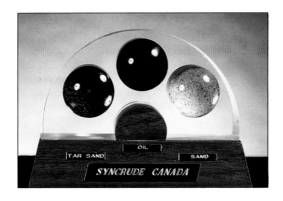

Oil sand display designed by Syncrude employee Jan Wonjo. Only 25 were made for presentation to touring V.I.P.s.

with leading the successful campaign to downsize the organization, trim production costs and improve safety and reliability .

Reminded later he was considered by many, "the best possible person for the times at the Syncrude helm," he smiled reticently and mused, "I wonder how many were

Ralph Shepherd
"Man of the Year"

saying that at the time!"

It seems many in the oil industry agreed. As testament to his contributions, the Alberta Chamber of Resources named him 1987s Man of the Year.

Although the Shepherds knew their stint in Fort McMurray was temporary, both were sorry to leave a city they describe as "a place of amazing vitality and energy — a friendly and open city that has everything you could imagine in the way of facilities."

TIPTOE THROUGH THE OIL SANDS

IN MARCH 1986, as the price of oil toppled and the province's economy crumbled, a moment of pure magic brought renewed animation to the site.

An Alberta government film crew arrived at the mine, with a delightful, petite ballerina and some burly actors in tow. She daintily pirouetted her way through this crowd of newly-minted workers, capturing a videotaped dream sequence on the Syncrude project for Canada's Expo '86 in Vancouver.

For a few moments on tape, the talented youngster brought an exquisite and ethereal character to an otherwise gritty world.

Perhaps it reminded some of the workers of the enchantment of the project that drew them to the north in the first place.

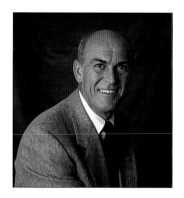

"IN 1986, THE CONVENTIONAL OILPATCH WAS A BLOODBATH. DRILLING STOPPED AND ALL OF THE SERVICE COMPANIES WERE GOING DOWN THE TUBES. WE SAW THE PRICE FOR SYNTHETIC CRUDE DROP FROM $45 (CANADIAN) A BARREL IN 1983-84 TO $15.25. BUT SOMEHOW SYNCRUDE MANAGED TO TRIM COSTS – AND WE SURVIVED!"

HARRY FORSTER, SYSTEMS ADVISOR,
FINANCIAL ACCOUNTING

In the fall of 1985, when budget restraint was being stressed, pressure of another kind caused the collapse of extraction's rejects conveyor, temporarily halting operations in the mine and extraction. Fortunately, no one was hurt in the incident. The company went on to celebrate a record-breaking year, producing 46.9 million barrels of synthetic crude oil at the lowest cash operating cost to date (less than $18 a barrel). This success was due in large part to debottlenecking, and improved worker safety.

GETTING IT UP FRONT

EARLY IN ITS PLANNING for expansion, Syncrude recognized the need to involve others in the process. Management decided on a novel approach. Rather than asking for public input after planning was complete, the company invited key stakeholders to participate up front — through an organization called the Syncrude Expansion Review Group (SERG).

Representatives of the general public, government regulatory agencies and the nearby community of Fort McKay met regularly to review plans, discuss environmental, socioeconomic and technical issues related to expansion, and work out agreements with the company on how public concerns would be met. Identified in a SERG report to the Energy Resources Conservation Board, these agreements were later reflected in the terms and conditions of ERCB approval.

Although an uncertain business climate has stalled the expansion program, Syncrude's refreshing approach to planning a major development has been adopted by others.

"To my knowledge, this was a first for Alberta," says Corporate Secretary Don Thompson. "At the time it was very unusual for a community such as Fort McKay to have direct up-front involvement in planning, without the need for an adversarial hearing process. In fact, the approach proved so successful it is becoming more and more common in industry."

A strong sense of foreboding, in early 1986, filled the air as world oil prices continued to plunge. The company was spending more than $20 Canadian per barrel to produce oil. This did not leave much margin to pay royalties, taxes and depreciation. Employees braced themselves for the financial blows and deprivations that would accompany layoffs; prices continued to wane.

Once again, people feared for their jobs and the company looked for alternative ways of dealing with the problem. The summer student program was eliminated. The 1986 budget

was slashed by a staggering $200 million. Two hundred contract workers were laid off, a freeze on hiring was imposed, spending on the Capacity Addition Project project was delayed and major cuts were made in all areas of the company.

Fortunately, employees also came to the rescue with hundreds of ideas which helped reduce cash operating costs to under $15 barrel, a new record which helped ensure the company's long-term viability.

By then, oil prices had hit a

"THE STRING OF NEW OIL SANDS PROJECTS ENVISIONED IN THE EARLY 1970S MAY NOT HAVE MATERIALIZED, BUT WE HAVE TO REMEMBER THAT THE GROWTH IN SYNCRUDE'S PRODUCTION DUE TO BOTH RELIABLE OPERATIONS AND THE AGGRESSIVE CAPITAL PROGRAM, HAS BEEN EQUIVALENT TO TWO NEW PROJECTS.

"WE ALSO HAVE TO REMEMBER THAT DESPITE THE ADJUSTMENTS YOU HAVE TO EXPECT AT START-UP, THIS HAS BEEN A PROFITABLE VENTURE. SYNCRUDE HAS PAID OVER $1 BILLION IN ROYALTIES AND MORE THAN $400 MILLION IN PROFITS TO THE HERITAGE SAVINGS TRUST FUND THROUGH ALBERTA OIL SANDS EQUITY. ALBERTA HAS ALSO GAINED EMPLOYMENT, COLLECTED TAXES FROM EMPLOYMENT AND BEEN ABLE TO PAY FOR AN INFRASTRUCTURE TO SUPPORT A CITY OF 35,000. ALL IN ALL, IT'S BEEN A GOOD DEAL!"

TOM VANT, CHAIRMAN, SYNCRUDE BOARD OF DIRECTORS,
AND CHAIRMAN, ALBERTA OIL SANDS EQUITY

THE OLYMPIC TORCH CAME TO FORT MCMURRAY, ON ITS WAY TO THE 1986 WINTER OLYMPIC GAMES IN CALGARY,

frightening low. Now sitting at an alarming $20 Canadian a barrel, the downward trend showed every sign of continuing and it did. The number of oil rigs working in Alberta plummeted.

Suncor was also hurting. The oil sands pioneer announced major layoffs and warned the entire operation might have to be dismantled if oil prices remained low.

Left: Although construction was delayed, the Capacity Addition Project would become a reality.

Below and centre left: Employee meetings with Ralph Shepherd led to new ideas for cost cutting.

99

"EVERY TIME YOU BUILD SOMETHING NEW, YOU PRESENT YOURSELF WITH AN OPPORTUNITY TO IMPROVE IT. FOR EXAMPLE, THE CAPACITY ADDITION PROJECT IN THE 1980S GAVE US MORE UPGRADING CAPACITY AND THAT PLACES TREMENDOUS PRESSURE ON EXTRACTION. SUDDENLY WE FACE ANOTHER RESEARCH CHALLENGE!"

THANE WALDIE, VICE PRESIDENT, TECHNOLOGY.

Below: A winter view of the Capacity Addition Project.

There were still islands of optimism while the death knell for the oil sands rang. The Other Six Lease Owners (OSLO) had been conducting geophysical and core exploration northeast of Fort MacKay for several years, and continued to do so. Although Syncrude's expansion plans had been shelved, they had not been discarded.

A provincial election was on the horizon and it seemed more than good timing when the province announced financial bailouts on the oil sands projects. Premier Don Getty promised to reduce royalties on Suncor's production and also offered loan guarantees to Syncrude to ensure construction of the CAP Project could continue, although it would be at a reduced rate.

But the economy demanded more definitive action. Syncrude was now losing over $5 dollars on every barrel of oil produced after crude prices dropped to $10 U.S. per barrel. For the first time in its history, Syncrude was forced to reduce its staff, largely through attrition. "Enhanced retirement packages" became a part of the vocabulary. "Long term leaves of

President Ralph Shepherd met with employees in 22 marathon meetings over six days.

absence" became acceptable. People in positions considered redundant were reassigned when possible and only a handful of layoffs occurred.

President Ralph Shepherd undertook a grueling schedule that allowed him to meet with employees in 22 marathon meetings over six days. He answered more than 1,300 questions about cost-cutting measures and how the company was dealing with this latest crisis.

The chairperson of the Independent Petroleum Association of Canada predicted 50 per cent or 55,000 jobs in the industry were at risk.

The workers at Suncor were also at odds with their company. A company lockout was followed by a long and bitter dispute that bordered on violence and fragmented the community. Rumors were rife; there was talk of martial law as the Royal Canadian Mounted Police struggled to tame a tempestuous, volatile situation.

Relief came in the form of crisis, an unexpected force that eliminated the barriers built by the labor brouhaha. A raging fire in the upgrading plant at Suncor brought the community together. Battle lines were forgotten as Suncor, Syncrude and city firefighters responded to the emergency. Though the cost of the fire hovered around

the $5 million mark, the tensions created by the strike eased somewhat.

After a stormy summer, Syncrude was again knocking on the doors of government, asking for loan guarantees to finish CAP. Alberta Energy Minister Neil Webber and Premier Don Getty talked to their federal counterparts about cost sharing. The federal government agreed to give the matter some thought.

Although the Premier was confident a deal could be struck, the federal government was slow to respond. Soon, Christmas hovered on the horizon, and with no response from Ottawa, Alberta's energy minister threatened to raise the drawbridge.

This would leave one of Syncrude's owners, Petro-Canada, out in the cold and out of the provincial loan scheme, if the province was left to finance the project.

"Auld acquaintances" generally saluted at the end of an old year and the beginning of a new, were cast aside when Marcel Masse, the federal minister of energy announced the government had already "...carried a disproportionate share of the financial burden" for the Syncrude plant and further financial assistance was not available.

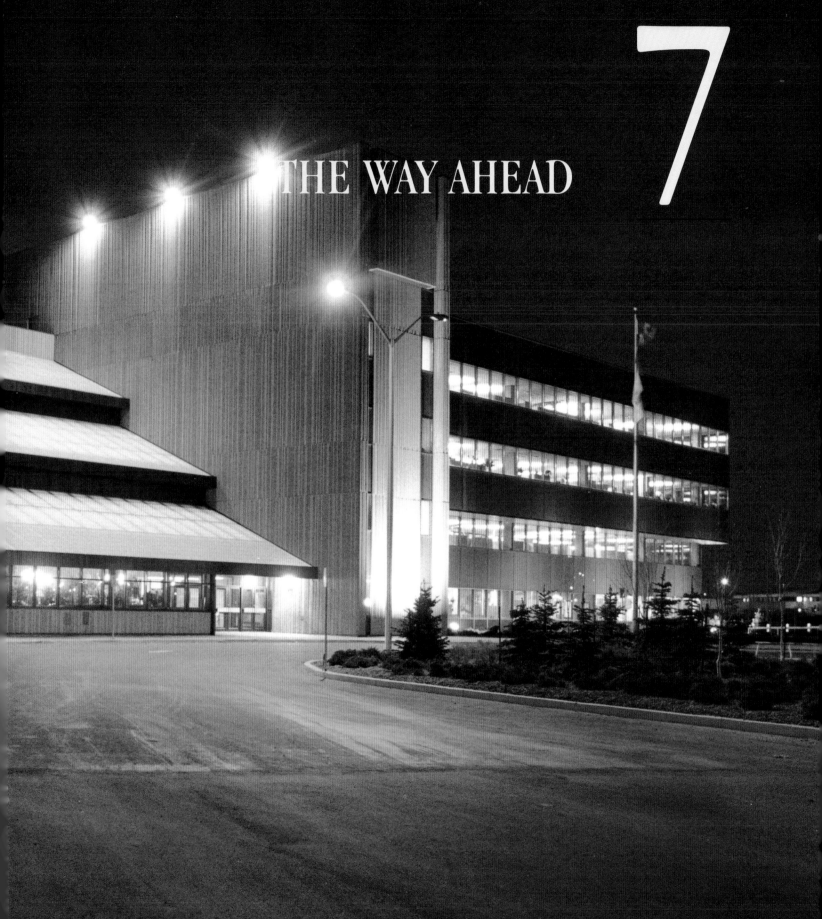

THE WAY AHEAD 7

Carbovan Inc. is now producing vanadium from fly ash.

While the political battle raged on, it was business as usual at the plant. A record breaking maintenance shutdown was carried out on coker 8-2 in a breathtaking 40 days and yet another new phrase emerged in the Syncrude vocabulary.

"Socio-tech" or sociotechnical redesign, became the method used to help reorganize work in utilities to get better results by giving people more responsibility for the tasks they performed. The overall premise of the approach was to create self-managing teams, with a clear product and business focus. Phil Lachambre, vice presi-dent, human resources notes: "In order to meet our business goals, we recognized that we needed to have employees in all areas of the operation taking initiative and responsibility for day-to-day decisions. We needed to give them the authority to make change happen and to achieve results".

The end of the decade has seen a growing awareness among employees of the need for change and continuous improvement in a business environment which is becoming increasingly competitive. As a result, new organization initiatives have been kicked off in all areas of the company, to improve on productivity and the quality of work life.

Change was also happening externally. Saudi Arabia came up with the "Triple 20" policy, which called for OPEC to limit oil production to 20 million barrels per day by the year 2000.

By 1987, the price of oil was on the rise again. A senior economist with the Energy Resources Conservation Board predicted the go ahead for three major oil sands projects if the price of oil reached levels of $25 U.S.

Fort McMurrayites got ready for another boom. Pre-engineering contracts for the expansion study were awarded and the community began to think in terms of another 5,000 taxpaying residents by 1993. The Alberta government assisted the expansion study by providing an $85 million dollar loan for engineering studies.

Plans for Carbovan Inc., a new plant that would produce vanadium, a trace metal used to strengthen metal, were also underway near Suncor. The federal and provincial govern-ments underscored their verbal support with an $8 million financial package.

Suncor also announced a $150 million expansion and debottlenecking project and everyone, including financial analysts, was confident the energy sector had gained its second wind.

But not for long. The first indication of trouble brewing on the horizon came when Finance Minister Michael Wilson introduced tax changes that would impact dramatically on new oil sands development. Gord Willmon, chairperson of Syncrude's management committee, hedged, saying "The changes require us to put up a lot more money at the front end." Ralph Shepherd voiced his concerns as well, adding: "So much risk is associated with expansion that our owners are unlikely to do anything unless it can be financed from cash flow from production. Expansion will probably take five years and our owners feel the government should defer tax and royalty revenues until the project is completed."

People power: Phil Lachambre, vice president, human resources, with Trudy Leddy (left) and Rhonda Carleton

Transporting extraction's inclined plate settler unit to the Syncrude site was a long and challenging trip – especially when corners had to be negotiated.

While a storm brewed over tax concessions and the financing of future oil sands development, Edmonton was ravaged by a tornado that tore a five kilometre wide path through the city's east end. Twenty-seven people died in the storm, another 250 were injured and millions of dollars of damage occurred in 30 minutes of unmerciful violence inflicted by nature.

Syncrude's research department, just blocks away from the eye of the violent storm, barely escaped the path of the tornado.

Both Syncrude and Suncor sent emergency response crews to assist their southern neighbor. They helped sift through the rubble and assisted with the cleanup of hazardous materials that had spilled predominantly in the industrial area.

ONE IN A HUNDRED

BY 1990, average annual staff turnover had dropped substantially from the early years to a little over seven per cent. This means that every year some 4,600 people continue working for Syncrude and opting for life in one of Canada's most vibrant and unusual industrial settings.

What keeps them on side? Human Resources, Vice President, Phil Lachambre cites some of the

reasons: the satisfaction of working as part of a team in a leading edge industry; good salary and benefits; excellent career development opportunities that help people expand their horizons and keep moving throughout the organization; the opportunity to be innovative and develop new technology; and company efforts to recognize achievement.

Syncrude has been listed in both editions of the Financial Post's "The Hundred Best Companies to Work for in Canada." Found under the category of "Challengers" in the most recent edition, Syncrude is rated as one of the best companies for pay, benefits, training, promotion and job security.

SHIFTING GEARS

THE DYNAMICS involved in keeping a plant like Syncrude operational 24 hours a day, require an elaborate, complex network of shift schedules to be sure the massive operation is always staffed and fully functional.

Enter the "shifters", the men and women who live their lives a step out of pace with the rest of the world. They leave for work when their families are heading for bed and get home just in time to kiss the kids goodbye on their way to school.

At Syncrude, shifters number in the thousands; for them, life is an endless array of cycles out of synch, but for many it is still a gratifying lifestyle. Steve Horsley (mining operations) says: "I sometimes don't even know what day of the week it is, but I know what shift I'm working, and I focus

Steve Horsley and family

Jack Lane relaxing with Pooh Bear after a long shift.

on that to keep myself organized." Jack Lane (automotive and support equipment services) concurs, adding, "Shifting is a life-style for most people who work shifts, though there are people whose biological clocks won't let them adapt to the changing schedules."

The spouses and families of most shiftworkers adjust as best they can. "I feel like I have all of the problems and none of the privileges of being a single mother," one said. "My husband is never here when something needs to be fixed, or one of the kids has to go in for stitches, and I don't remember the last time we went out for an evening together. There are times when I really hate it... I'd just like my family to live like everyone else, 9 to 5."

Near the end of 1987, Ralph Shepherd once again called employees together, this time bearing good tidings. The news – the company produced about three million barrels more than expected and costs were averaging about 50 cents a barrel less than in 1986 – gave reason for a great deal of cautious optimism.

"Last year we were in very difficult times, but through the efforts of employees we were able to make the kind of gains necessary to survive. We now know the talent is out there to work toward a new prosperity in the oil patch," Shepherd explained.

In January 1988, Energy Minister Neil Webber announced the development of the OSLO project would be preferable to the Syncrude expansion, because OSLO had the potential to create more jobs. While the six OSLO partners are also a part of the Syncrude consortium, the projects were in competition. The federal government's

Process Technician John Malcolm, making instrument adjustments during one of his shifts.

immediate response was to establish a review committee to study megaproject proposals.

The course of Syncrude's progress took yet another turn when the company, intent on hiring almost 500 employees to fill positions caused by turnover and the startup of CAP units, discovered a large portion of applicants could not meet company hiring standards.

After reviewing the problem, and its implications for future hiring, the company introduced a minimum grade 12 equivalency requirement and also added special pre-employment tests for entry-level candidates.

Later the same year, the company created an internship position for Michael Cachia, a local high school teacher, to conduct a special research project for the Alberta Foundation for Economic Education to help find ways to incorporate aspects of the company's business operation for possible use in the curriculum in Alberta schools.

BUREAUCRACY BUSTERS

IN THE ON-GOING BATTLE to drive down operating costs, Syncrude spawned a new type of soldier in the 1980s. Called the "Bureaucracy Busters", this elite troop consists of pragmatic staff members who see the value in working smarter, not harder.

They're the people who see ways to cut down on red tape by such simple steps as eliminating unneeded copies of documents, questioning the need for bulky reports that nobody reads, or simplifyng stock management procedures.

"The individual savings don't have to be dramatic to add up to millions of dollars over the life of the project," explains Ray Beswick, project leader, management control/bureaucracy reduction program. "We thought of establishing a central reporting system to keep track of the savings – but decided against it when we realized we'd be adding to the bureaucratic burden."

As 1988 drew to a close, oil prices again began to fluctuate dramatically. The oil industry took the swings of the pricing pendulum in stride, taking a "business as usual" approach to the situation. That year the company broke the 50 million barrel mark, setting its third consecutive production record in as many years.

Problems with the new hydrocracker, a fire and a labor dispute marked the final months of 1988.

In early 1989, John Lynn, Syncrude's former president and chief executive officer, was named project executive for the OSLO project. Less than six months later, the future of the consortium was in question, because of high interest rates. The people of Fort McMurray suspected it might be another Alsands pipedream.

As had frequently occurred in the past, when everything appeared bleak, an unrelated event took place which changed the focus of attention.

That spring the entire world riveted its attention on a tiny inlet on the west coast of Alaska, where a massive oil tanker, loaded with millions of gallons of oil, spilled 20 per cent of its cargo into waters off the Atlantic Ocean. The

In early fall of 1987, the last of 269 modules for CAP arrived; the project was completed three months ahead of schedule and came in under budget by a staggering $40 million. The savings were attributed in large part to "... the efficiencies the people building CAP discovered as they went along."

Left: Construction of a T.O.R. unit.

Below: The Tailings Oil Recovery Unit (T.O.R.) developed by Luba Cymbalisty and George Cymerman, removes bitumen from tailings sand that plant 5 cannot. This accounts for an additional 10 to 15 thousand barrels of bitumen recovered per day.

damage was extensive, the reaction intense.

Environmental awareness became environmental action. A new age of respect for the ecosystem was born and Syncrude was caught right in the middle in March 1989, when a near disaster followed close on the heels of the oil spill.

Due to an undetected leak of a toxic chemical (from a supplier's container being transported by an independent trucking company), 30 kilometres of highway mid-way between Edmonton and Fort McMurray had to be closed for clean up.

Syncrude, consistent with its loss management principles, undertook additional actions beyond its legal requirements, to prevent a similar incident in the future.

The events of late spring were followed by an illegal walkout of building trades people. This protest by employees of a major contractor halted most of the maintenance work on one of the cokers that summer. After six days of negotiations, and a back to work order from the Alberta Labour Relations Board, work on the coker resumed.

In August 1989, Ralph Shepherd, the man who had held the reins during some of the oil sand industry's most turbulent years, was about to dismount from the saddle. His ability to manage a complex operation as well as to help the company achieve its highest production levels at the lowest production costs ever, earned him the admiration and affection of all.

PLANE DOWN

THE DRAMA OF CONTROVERSY over federal government involvement in the project was somewhat diminished when Syncrude's corporate twin-engine turboprop crashed in dense brush and darkness, near the Fort McMurray airport on December 10, 1986. Miraculously, the pilot, co-pilot and two passengers survived. The wings of the craft were sheared off, however, and the aircraft was totally destroyed.

Plant 22-1, the hydrocracker, performs a similar function to the cokers but uses more advanced technology.

CAPACITY ADDITION FEVER

SYNCRUDE'S 10TH anniversary of operation was marked by the start-up of CAP, which Thane Waldie, Syncrude's vice-president of technology described as "... a significant milestone in Syncrude's progress since CAP utilizes process technology that could be the basis for future expansion."

The occasion was marked by grand celebrations, including a special ceremony at Mildred Lake, attended by no less than 300 people from throughout North America

including several cabinet ministers. The Premier and deputy Prime Minister were noticeably absent, which fueled rumors that the Syncrude expansion was in jeopardy, despite the company's ability to start the

project almost immediately.

The governments were, it seemed, prepared to rain on the anniversary parade.

First, at a giant press conference that attracted local, regional and national media, they announced their support, of the OSLO project. On the heels of that announcement, the Premier revealed his intention to raise $500 million from the sale of Syncrude shares to use as an investment in OSLO. The proposed expansion was shelved.

Left: Super Saturday, a combination of CAP opening and a celebration of 10 years of production, proved to be fun for all.

Below: Erection of the reactors in plant 22 takes place using special cranes.

Some of the song contestants became popular performers at site functions. From left are: Robin Penner, Paul Scanlon, Ed Kaine, Debra Elliot, and Chas O'Hanley.

STAR SEARCH

(excerpted from a 1988 TIP article)
by Shelley Shehinski

SYNCRUDE CELEBRATES 10 YEARS WITH AMATEUR SONGWRITING TALENT!

Syncrude has become a hot topic in unofficial songwriting history after the Star Search songwriting contest, celebrating our 10 years of production.

From mourning a hometown left behind and insights into riding our daily buses, to keeping the kids quiet for a shiftworking Dad and cheering for DDOs; roughly 75 entrants detailed their thoughts on Syncrude with new lyrics for existing songs.

One entry was a singing job application while others wrote their own words and music, or actually recorded their efforts for the judges.

And for the winners, most of whom admittedly have scant musical talent, there is nothing finer than being honoured for their debut attempts at lyrical success.

For Dave Sibley, who's not a bit musical, his incredibly detailed lyrics for The Syncrude Canada Trilogy, based on the tune of Gordon Lightfoot's Canadian Railroad Trilogy, netted him first place in the individual Syncrude employee category.

Pat Thompson, who won in the best community members category, composed Onward Driver—Off to Syncrude to the unlikely tune of the Battle Hymn of the Republic. Try marching to this first verse:

Mine eyes have seen the glory
Of the coming of my bus.
The driver nods his greeting
And I board without a fuss.
I take my seat and settle in
His driving I can trust.
And Syncrude's where we go.

Harry Boone and Barb Musey composed Once Upon a Time based on Those Were the Days My Friend. Hum the chorus to these words:

Syncrude's been good to us
They take us on that bus
To work all day and
*   some to work at night*
The money's good you see
It buys my toys for me
I've done OK, oh yes I've done
*   alright*
La, la, la, la, la, la . . .

Boone, a heavy duty mechanic in mine mobile, says the song is really a tribute to the employees who have stuck with Syncrude throughout the years. "We just wanted to say that Syncrude is a great company."

Writing a song between periods in a hockey game netted The Syncrude Boogie a first prize for the best original song and lyrics, explains winning team member Ed "Leadbelly" Kaine, section head, extraction/primary upgrading technical services.

The team, self-named Men With Hardhats, have spawned a small fan club after two performances of their original 12-bar blues tribute to the company at the summer Syncrude barbeque. Donning Syncrude hardhats, Kaine, Geoff "Blues" Pearson, Paul "Elwood" Scanlon, Robin "Jake" Penner and "Magic" Chas O'Hanley thrilled the crowd with such lyrics as:

Draglines and bucketwheels,
*   conveyors by the mile*
Send tarsand to the pocket,
*   and dump it all in piles*
Tumblers and separators,
*   they're running all the*
*   while*
50 million barrels is
*   where we set the dial . . .*

"We felt that the words fit the occasion. It's a positive tune even though it was to a bluesy beat," says Kaine. The song was recorded by technical and musical wizard Geoff Pearson.

The contest's youngest

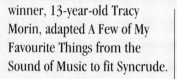

Syncrude's Super Saturday event in Heritage Park. Men With Hardhats perform The Syncrude Boogie.

winner, 13-year-old Tracy Morin, adapted A Few of My Favourite Things from the Sound of Music to fit Syncrude.

Tarsand on work boots and
thick safety glasses,
Noisy machinery and
weird smelling gasses,
Turkey and lettuce for lunch
if you please,
These are a few of my favour-
ite things.

Tracy dedicated the song to her father, Mike Bazinet, extraction, team four, based on things he tells her about Syncrude. True to a budding songwriter's needs, Tracy plans on buying an electric typewriter with the contest prize money.

Team one, equipment services, won as best Syncrude team with the tune Syncrude on My Mind based on an Elvis Presley song, The Promised Land. Don E. Gordon wrote the lyrics with the encouragement of the rest of the team.

Other members of the winning team are: Dave Harris, Gordon Bird, Barrie McKitrick, Scott Canning, Ray Labelle, Peter Brenders, Niel Vanbrowershaven, Bill Sloboda and Grenville Cullihall.

"I knew Syncrude was looking for a theme so I based the song on someone coming here 10 years ago and the people from Newfoundland who left their home from a great distance."

I left my home in Grand
Bank, Newfoundland
Alberta on my mind
Riding through the Klondike
city
Atlantic waters far behind
When I was young I looked to
sea
The roll of the surging tide
The salty mist is distant now
I'm on the other side

Barbara Bellemare, community relations, says she wasn't sure how the contest was going to work because nothing like it had ever been attempted at Syncrude.

"The fact that we got more than 75 entries shows that people are open to new ideas and if given the opportunity, they'll do it. A lot of the songs were written from the heart."

Entrants became personally involved with the contest and took a sense of ownership by, in many cases, writing about their work area, she says.

"We heard more from occupational employees, people in operations, than anywhere else on site. You can really learn something by reading these songs," says Bellemare.

See if you learn something by tapping your toes along with these popular tunes put to Syncrude words:

"Well nothing could be
finer than to be a Syncrude
miner in the morning. Noth-
ing is much sweeter than to
hear a back-up tweeter in the
morning," by Peter Rudiak.

Or a version of Alabama's "40 hour week" by Ray Klem, upgrading technical, which covered the whole plant and most of the workers in it.

This is for the one who drives
the heavy haulers,
Up and down the road
For the one out in the ware-
house
Bringing in the load
For the administrator, the
mechanic
The process operator on
patrol

For the programmer, the
electrician
Who reads the secret code
For everyone who works
behind the scene
With a spirit you can't
replace with no machine

Or how about dancing to the Tarsand Rock (to the tune of the Elvis Presley classic Jailhouse Rock, by human resources table 3 following a departmental meeting;):

Ralph threw a party
down at Mildred Lake,
The Raven Band was there
and they began to shake.
The cokers were jumping and
the site began to swing.
You should have heard the
owners when the phones
began to ring.

The United Way Campaign is always a big event at Syncrude. Here staff of the communications division along with Vice President, Human Resources, Phil Lachambre display the meal they prepared to raise United Way funds.

ERIC NEWELL

HE'S A YOUTHFUL, affable and gentle man committed to the community he lives in and his company. At 45, Eric Newell, president and chief executive officer of Alberta's largest private sector employer, is the veritable "new kid on the block" when it comes to length of service with Syncrude, but a seasoned veteran when one considers his career within the petroleum industry as a whole.

A chemical engineer with a master's of science degree in management studies, Newell's professional life has been

Eric Newell

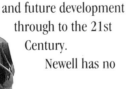

a nomadic one. His resume reads like a road map of Canada, with red dots in such cities as Toronto, Vancouver, Montreal, Sarnia and Dartmouth; indeed Fort McMurray marks his 15th major move in 20 years.

He is firm in the conviction that his tenure in Alberta's Oil Sands Country will be more than temporary. This is not simply because Fort McMurray is the place his family calls "home" but because he is dedicated to the oil sands and determined to see its progress and future development through to the 21st Century.

Newell has no

illusions about the ramifications of such a decision and says it is imperative to plan today for the changes of tomorrow. "It's urgent that we do it now. The world marketplace is changing so rapidly, we no longer have the luxury of clinging to the traditional ways of doing business".

Newell, who has, on occasion, good-naturedly introduced himself as "Papa Smurf" (due to his bantam stature), has a clear picture of what he wants for the company, and the world by the end of the decade.

"In the short term, we have to reduce costs and narrow the gap between our production costs and those for conventional crude oil. We've traveled a long road already, if you include finding costs for conventional crude oil (our finding costs are zero) and our total costs are within $5 per barrel of conventional oil and we are rapidly closing the gap. We have to demonstrate once and for all that oil sands development is Canada's best choice to meet Canada's energy requirements. I know we can do it, if we work as a team."

This spirit is the philosophy behind the company's vision statement, which states that Syncrude's major thrust will be to: *"Secure Canada's energy future with the vision to lead, the knowledge to succeed, the commitment to do better and the heart to win the race."*

In many respects, Newell demonstrates the same vision, commitment and heart as that of his predecessor, Frank Spragins, although the suggestion of the parallels between the two men leaves Newell slightly uncomfortable.

"Frank Spragins was an industry giant. While he may

Right: 1990's celebration in Edmonton.

Members (1990):

Margaret Parnham
Norman Fong
Cliff Paton
Lubomyr (Luba) Cymbalisty
Ronald Gray
Kermit Haakonson
Charles Hall
Al Hyndman
Vic Kaminsky
Gordon Thompson
Marciano Baptista
Walter Rilkoff
Nicholas Salzl
George Williamson

Corner left: The Newell family at home in Fort McMurray.

Ron Gray, Quarter Century Club member gives a "thumbs up" sign to the future of Syncrude.

have been considered tough, he was a consummate gentleman whose incredible conviction and faith gave life to the oil sands."

One senses, in just a few years, Newell himself may be described in like terms. He's a man of today, with a tenacious grasp on tomorrow. "I think the year 2000 may see at least one more grass roots oil sands plant, and perhaps another on the way. But I feel new projects may take new directions. Rather than being totally integrated facilities, we'll utilize existing and emerging technologies to separate some of the functions such as mining and extraction from upgrading."

And like millions of others around the world, Newell is convinced industry will have to respond more efficiently and effectively to environmental issues. "Right from the start, Frank Spragins made a commitment, on behalf of the company, to reclaim the land we mine and even improve on its original condition. Our commitment to this principle remains unchanged. Syncrude has been at the forefront, not only in safety, reliability, environmental improvements and technology, but also in areas such as organizational design, human resource policies and business ethics. We've overcome a multitude of problems in the past and we're a lot older and smarter now. We have to take our knowledge and experience and use it for the good of not just the company, but also for the local community, the province and the country as a whole."

QUARTER CENTURY CLUB

IN THE BEGINNING, they were young, and the 21st century seemed little more than an imaginary cloud on a far-off horizon.

Today, their hair is streaked with silver, or in a few cases, no longer there. But the energy, excitement and commitment they first brought to the oil sands continues.

In September, 1989, Syncrude established a "Quarter Century Club" for those employees who had been with the company at least 25 years, to honor and thank them for their courage, conviction and unequivocal support.

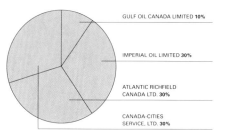

ONTARIO ENERGY
CORPORATION **5%**

ROYALITE OIL COMPANY
LIMITED **10%**

GULF OIL CANADA LIMITED **10%**

HER MAJESTY THE QUEEN
IN RIGHT OF THE PROVINCE
OF ALBERTA **10%**

HER MAJESTY THE QUEEN
IN RIGHT OF CANADA **15%**

IMPERIAL OIL LIMITED **30%**

IMPERIAL OIL LIMITED **30%**

GULF OIL CANADA
LIMITED **16.75%**

RICHFIELD OIL CORPORATION **30%**

ATLANTIC RICHFIELD
CANADA LTD. **30%**

CANADA-CITIES
SERVICE, LTD. **22%**

CITIES SERVICE
ATHABASCA, INC. **30%**

CANADA-CITIES
SERVICE, LTD. **30%**

IMPERIAL OIL LIMITED **31.25%**

SYNCRUDE
BOARD OF DIRECTORS

T.R. Vant
Chairman of the Board

Robert Fischer
MLA

Roger D. Dunn
Vice President
Alberta Energy Company Ltd.
Calgary, Alberta

Vincent J. Gallant
Comptroller
Alberta Energy Company Ltd.
Calgary, Alberta

Charles R. Mikkelborg
Senior Vice President
Canadian Occidental Petroleum Ltd.
Calgary, Alberta

Waleed Jazrawi

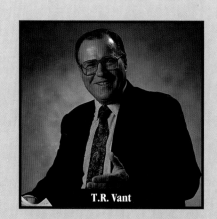

T.R. Vant

"I REMEMBER IN MANY EARLY MEETINGS,
DICK GALBREATH OF CITIES SERVICE
WOULD POINT OUT THAT WE SEEMED TO BE
GETTING OFF THE TRACK. HE WOULD SAY:
'DON'T FORGET WHY WE'RE DOING THIS
PROJECT, WE'RE DOING IT FOR THE
PEOPLE.' THEN SOMEBODY WOULD SAY,
'THAT'S JUST OLD DICK BEING HOKEY
AGAIN.' BUT THEN HE'D REPEAT IT — AND IN
THE END WE ALL KNEW IT WAS TRUE.
PEOPLE FELT THIS WAS A VERY IMPORTANT
PROJECT AND THEY WANTED TO DO IT
RIGHT. IT'S STILL IMPORTANT AND THAT
FEELING HAS SURVIVED."

TOM VANT, CHAIRMAN, SYNCRUDE BOARD OF DIRECTORS,
AND CHAIRMAN, ALBERTA OIL
SANDS EQUITY

J. Angus McKee
President and CEO
Canadian Occidental Petroleum Ltd.
Calgary, Alberta

Waleed Jazrawi
Athabasca Manager
Esso Resources Canada Limited
Calgary, Alberta

Gordon J. Willmon
Vice President and Director
Esso Resources Canada Limited
Calgary, Alberta

W. Glen Russell
Vice President, Major Projects
Gulf Canada Resources Limited
Calgary, Alberta

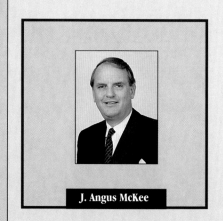

J. Angus McKee

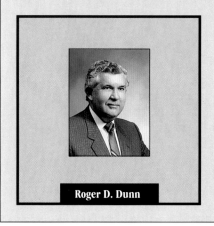

Roger D. Dunn

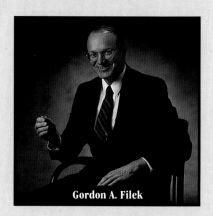

Gordon A. Filek

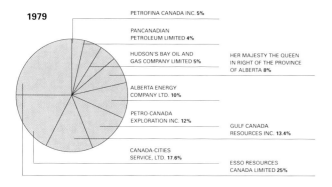

1979

PETROFINA CANADA INC. **5%**

PANCANADIAN PETROLEUM LIMITED **4%**

HUDSON'S BAY OIL AND GAS COMPANY LIMITED **5%**

HER MAJESTY THE QUEEN IN RIGHT OF THE PROVINCE OF ALBERTA **8%**

ALBERTA ENERGY COMPANY LTD. **10%**

PETRO-CANADA EXPLORATION INC. **12%**

GULF CANADA RESOURCES INC. **13.4%**

CANADA-CITIES SERVICE, LTD. **17.6%**

ESSO RESOURCES CANADA LIMITED **25%**

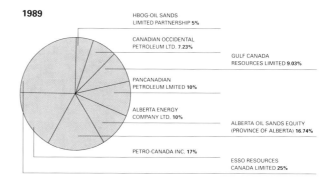

1989

HBOG-OIL SANDS LIMITED PARTNERSHIP **5%**

CANADIAN OCCIDENTAL PETROLEUM LTD. **7.23%**

GULF CANADA RESOURCES LIMITED **9.03%**

PANCANADIAN PETROLEUM LMITED **10%**

ALBERTA ENERGY COMPANY LTD. **10%**

ALBERTA OIL SANDS EQUITY (PROVINCE OF ALBERTA) **16.74%**

PETRO-CANADA INC. **17%**

ESSO RESOURCES CANADA LIMITED **25%**

Bob H. Scott
Manager, Major Projects Planning
Gulf Canada Resources Limited
Calgary, Alberta

Gordon A. Filek
Manager, Division Joint Interest
HBOG Oil Sands Limited Partnership
Calgary, Alberta

Murray B. Todd
Senior Vice President
Production and Development
HBOG Oil Sands Limited Partnership
Calgary, Alberta

Thomas R. Vant
Chairman
Alberta Oil Sands Equity
Edmonton, Alberta

Gordon J. Willmon

"SO MUCH OF THE BOTTOM LINE SUCCESS OF SYNCRUDE DEPENDS ON OIL PRICES, WHICH MEANS THAT OVER THE PAST 12 YEARS OF PRODUCTION WE HAVE HAD SOME VERY GOOD YEARS AND SOME VERY BAD YEARS. ON BALANCE I THINK THE VENTURE HAS BEEN MORE PROFITABLE THAN ESSO ORIGINALLY ANTICIPATED. AND WITH THE CONVENTIONAL WISDOM THAT OIL PRICES WILL GO UP, WE THINK IT WILL BE EVEN MORE PROFITABLE IN FUTURE."

GORDON WILLMON, CHAIRMAN, SYNCRUDE MANAGEMENT COMMITTEE, AND VICE PRESIDENT, ESSO RESOURCES CANADA LIMITED

Rich C. Verner
Executive Vice President
PanCanadian Petroleum Limited
Calgary, Alberta

Kenneth B. Cusworth
Senior Vice President, Corporate
PanCanadian Petroleum Limited
Calgary, Alberta

James M. Stanford
Chief Operating Officer
Petro-Canada Inc.
Calgary, Alberta

Jim Pantelidis
President
Petro-Canada Resources
Calgary, Alberta

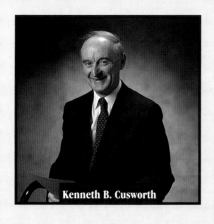

Kenneth B. Cusworth

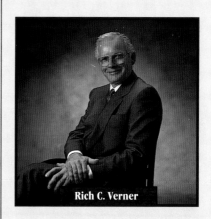

Rich C. Verner

Bob H. Scott

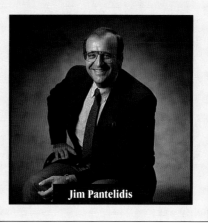

Jim Pantelidis

Whatever happens to Syncrude, the one constant has been a spirit of willingness to overcome adversity, setbacks and obstacles. Jim Carter, vice president, operations is optimistic about tomorrow.

He sees a future where Syncrude will continue to set new production records; and be an innovator in new oil sand technology, while at the same time containing costs in one of the safest working environments in the country.

"I believe we can generate the kind of cash flow to our owners that will make Syncrude an attractive investment for them, while Syncrude employees become the world's recognized authority on oil sands plant development and operations."

Fort McMurray has also become one of the premier resource cities in the country with some of the finest recreational and educational facilities available in a city with a 35,000 population.

But while the region has long-since cast off its cocoon, the spirit of adventure and pioneering which called people to the North, and to Oil Sands Country, continues.

For it is in the North that Canada's energy future is being written...and in the oils sands industry, safety, technology and development reign supreme.

Credits

Photos are listed for each page in a clockwise direction from the top left.

Cover photo, Ian Biggar
Dedication page, Luba Cymbalisty
1. *(contents)*, Victor Post
2-3. Brenda Bastell
4. University of Alberta Archives, University of Alberta Archives
5. Glenbow Alberta Archives, Historic Sites Service Alberta Culture
6. Syncrude Communications, Syncrude Communications, Syncrude Communications
7. Oil Sands Interpretive Centre, Oil Sands Interpretive Centre, Syncrude Communications
8. Michael Shimbashi, Royal Canadian Geographic Society, Syncrude Communications, Public Archives Canada
9. Historic Sites Service-Alberta Culture, Syncrude Communications, Westfile (background)
10. Syncrude Communications, Oil Sands Interpretive Centre, Syncrude Communications, Syncrude Communications
11. Victor Post, Brenda Bastell, Oil Sands Interpretive Centre
12. Walter Rilkoff (background), Brenda Bastell, Michael Shimbashi
13. Michael Shimbashi, Michael Shimbashi
14. Syncrude Communications, Shelley Shehinski
15. Oil Sands Interpretive Centre, Syncrude Communications
17. Oil Sands Interpretive Centre, Warren Clark, Westfile
18. Syncrude Communications
20. Warren Clark
21. Syncrude Communications
22. Victor Post, Victor Post
23. Warren Clark, Sandra Daley
24-25. Ian Biggar
26. Ian Biggar
27. Victor Post, Floyd Aaring

28. Brenda Bastell, Syncrude Communications
29. Aurel Langevin, Oil Sands Interpretive Centre, Aurel Langevin, Victor Post
30. Victor Post, Syncrude Communications
31. Aurel Langevin, John Culliton, Premay Equipment Ltd., Ian Biggar
32. Warren Clark, Victor Post, Ian Biggar, Victor Post
33. Warren Clark, Syncrude Communications, Victor Post
34. Field and Field, Alex Sawer, Syncrude Communications
35. Ian Biggar, Syncrude Communications, Brenda Bastell, Brenda Bastell
36. Syncrude Communications, Syncrude Communications, Warren Clark
38. Phylice Barry, Brenda Bastell
38-39. Ian Biggar
40. Brenda Bastell, Syncrude Communications
41. Syncrude Communications, Warren Clark
42. Westfile, Syncrude Communications
44. Warren Clark, Westfile
45. Ian Biggar, Warren Clark
46. Syncrude Communications, Syncrude Communications
47. Ian Biggar
48. Michael Shimbashi, Aurel Langevin, Richard Siemens
49. Ian Biggar, Ian Biggar, Syncrude Communications
50. Syncrude Communications, Ian Biggar, Ian Biggar, Alex MacDonald
51. Warren Clark, John Culliton
52. Victor Post, Ernest Houle, Ian Biggar
53. Alan Schietzsch, Syncrude Communications, Ian Biggar
54-55. Victor Post
56. Ian Biggar, Warren Clark
57. Brenda Bastell, Syncrude Communications
58. Ken Kilburn, Warren Clark, Dale Toogood

59. Syncrude Communications, Syncrude Communications
60. Brenda Bastell, Victor Post
61. Westfile, Syncrude Communications, Ranson
62. Paul Hrabec, Paul Hrabec, Warren Clark
63. Syncrude Communications, Syncrude Communications
64. Stan McQuitty, Syncrude Communications
65. Victor Post, Shell Canada Resources Ltd.
66. Ken and Leita Hayward
67. Syncrude Communications, Syncrude Communications
68. Virginia Medleylane, Syncrude Communications, Westfile, Westfile
69. Ian Biggar, Syncrude Communications
70-71. Ian Biggar
72. Brenda Bastell, Victor Post, Westfile
73. Victor Post;
74. Syncrude Communications
75. Richard Siemens (background)
76. Syncrude Communications, Syncrude Communications
77. Syncrude Communications, Syncrude Communications, Richard Siemens
78. Syncrude Communications;
79. Syncrude Communications, Richard Siemens
80. Syncrude Communications, Syncrude Communications, Syncrude Communications
81. Nancy Grenier, Palson, Palson
82. Shelley Shehinski, Jody MacPherson, Syncrude Communications
83. Shelley Shehinski, Ian Biggar, Ian Biggar, Victor Post
84. Syncrude Communications, Syncrude Communications;
85. Ian Biggar, Dennis Lewandoski, Richard Siemens
86-87. Victor Post
88. Ian Biggar, Syncrude, Barbara Bellemare
89. Syncrude, Syncrude
90. Syncrude Communications, Victor Post, Syncrude

91. Gisela Love, Gerry Rasmussen, Syncrude
92. Syncrude Communications, Westfile, Victor Post. Syncrude Communications
93. Nancy Grenier, Ian Biggar, Ian Biggar, Victor Post
94. John Cooper, John Luckhurst, John Luckhurst, Brenda Bastell (background)
95. John Cooper, John Luckhurst, Karo, Karo
96. Syncrude Communications, Syncrude Communications, Elsie Velvick
97. Ted Shehinski, Greg Coyes, Syncrude Communications
98. Brenda Bastell, Syncrude Communications
99. Syncrude Communications, Jody MacPherson, Syncrude Communications, Barbara Bellemare
100. Brenda Bastell, Syncrude Communications
101. Syncrude Communications;
102-103. Ian Biggar
104. Brenda Bastell, Brenda Bastell
105. Jody MacPherson, Ian Biggar;
106. Virginia Medleylane, Steve Horsley
107. Syncrude Communications, Warren Clark
108. Luba Cymbalisty, Luba Cymbalisty
109. Victor Post, Victor Post, Eric Gordon
110. Syncrude Communications, Ian Biggar
111. Syncrude Communications
112. Syncrude Communications, Brenda Bastell
113. Syncrude Communications, Syncrude Communications, Michael Shimbashi
114. Brian Harder, Angus McKee, Brian Harder, Syncrude Communications, Brian Harder
115. Brian Harder, Brian Harder, Brain Harder, Syncrude Communications, Brian Harder
116-117. Ian Biggar

LEIGHTON VALERE LEIGHTON KENNETH LEINWEBER ROBERT LEISHMAN GILBERT LEMAY LAURENCE LEMESURIER GAETAN LEMIEUX ARTHUR W. LEMKE MARGARET W. LEMMON HELEN LEMOY WILLIAM N. LENNIE DAVID WILLIAM LENNON JAMES V. LENT EDWARD LENTOWICZ MURRAY E LENYK JOYCE E. LEONARD STEPHEN LEONARD ALBERT LEONG LOKE MUN LEONG SEK-MUN LEONG SHUI-HING LEONG ROY A. LEPINE ANTHONY C. LEROUX BERNARD LEROUX DONALD LEROUX GEORGE L LESKO BRYAN LESLIE RAY J LESLIE NORMAN LETAIN JUDY E LETOURNEAU MAURICE A LETOURNEAU ROBERT F LETOURNEAU AMELIA LEUNG DAVID LEUNG DR. ANTONY LEUNG HAROLD LEVERRE DENIS B. LEVERT CHARLES LEVESQUE GUILDO LEVESQUE MONTE LEVOIR DENNIS LEWANDOSKI JOE LEWIS SCOTT LEWIS TERRANCE P LEWIS NEIL LHIRONDELLE CECIL LI HIN HERN (BOB) LIANG ALFRED H.F. LIAO HARVEY LIDKEA RONALD G. LIDSTONE BARRY A. LIEN KARL H LIETZ CHEE WEE LIEW HON LIEW LEO LIEW MARY LIEW WALTER LINASSI CANDICE LINCK ROSS J. LINDENBERGER DAN LINES MARTIN LINES ORSON A T LINTON HEIDI LIPPERT LIONEL LISHCHYNSKY BEAT R. LIST JAMES E LITTLE RICHARD T LITTLE CHRISTINE LITTLETON BORIS E. LITWIN DR. JOSEPH K LIU QUENTIN W. LIZOTTE REES LLEWELLYN ANDREW LLOYD DONNA LLOYD RICHARD LLOYD STEPHEN LLOYD SUSAN LLOYD WILLIAM A. LLOYD CHARLES LO KOO FU LO PETER LO ANNA LOADER ROBERT LOADER GERALD D LOBB ANN LOCKE JIM LOCKE MORGAN LOCKYER WILFRED LOCKYER DARREN A. LODER DEXTER LODER MERVIN LODER RAYMOND C. LODER CLARK A LOGAN DAWN LOGAN ROBERT LOGAN ROY G. LOGAN STERLING LOGGIE FOH F LOH JAN LOIMAND BRIAN LOKHORST LYNN LOKOS TODD LONEY DONNA LONG PERRY LONG GARY S LONGHURST ANTHONY W.C. LOO CHARLOTTE LOO TED J LOPATYNSKI ALVARO LOPES EDWARD R F LORD LOUIS LORD MARLENE LORD GORDON R. LORENZ KEVIN LORETTE MICHAEL J. LORIMER MICHELE L LOSIER ARNOLD LOUGHEED ALLAN R. LOUTITT DENNIS E. LOVE JAY LOVE DOUGLAS S. LOVEGROVE JERRY LOVELESS RODERICK W. LOVELESS KOK THEN LOW DAVID S. LOWE EVANS LOWE DAVID J. LOWER IAN LOWTHER LOUIS M. LUCAS MARGARET R. LUCHAK CARSON R. LUCK ROBERT E. LUCK HELEN LUEDEE IRENE J. LUEDEE C.NEIL LUND ROBERT A LUND EVELYN LUNDQUIST ANN LUNGUL TERRANCE P. LUPIEN YVES-RENE LUPIEN WALTER LUPRYPA DALE LUSH HAROLD LUSH JIM LUSH JOHN CHARLES LUSH LAWRENCE LUSH PAUL J. LUSH RANDY LUSTIG TAN LUU ARMAND LYNCH DANIEL LYNCH ROBERT LYNCH DON LYNEM JOSEPH A LYNK PETER A. LYNN R.GRANT LYONS EDGAR MA HANS G. MAAS ROLAND MAAS DONALD P. MACALLISTER ROBERT M. MACAULAY BRYAN MACDONALD CAROL R MACDONALD CHRISTELLA MACDONALD DAN F. MACDONALD FRASER MACDONALD J BRENTON MACDONALD J. BRIAN MACDONALD J. RONALD MACDONALD JASON B. MACDONALD JOAN MACDONALD JOHN MACDONALD JOSEPH MACDONALD KENNETH B. MACDONALD TERRANCE J. MACDONALD THOMAS M. MACDONALD WAYNE E MACDONALD WILLIAM D MACDONALD CELENE MACDONELL STANLEY J MACDONELL DAVID G. MACDONNELL HUGHIE MACDOUGALL RONALD MACEACHERN PAULALINE MACGILLIVRAY ROGER D. MACGILLIVRAY DEAN O.M. MACGOUGAN ROBERT M. MACGREGOR BLANKA MACHALKA JAN MACHALKA WALDEMAR MACIEJEWSKI DANIEL J. MACISAAC MARY MACISAAC BRIAN MACK EDWARD A. MACKAY JAMES MACKEIGAN MARGUERITE MACKEIGAN DALE MACKENZIE VALERIE MACKENZIE WILLIAM A. MACKENZIE AMBROSE MACKEY ARTHUR MACKIE BRENT MACKINNON CAREY G MACKINNON GEORGE MACKINNON MAREN MACKINNON MICHAEL MACKINNON RUSSELL MACKINNON RICHARD MACKINTOSH JOHN J MACKWOOD GARNET L. MACLACHLAN IAN MACLACHLAN ALPHONSE J. MACLEAN GERALDINE MACLEAN JAMES P. MACLEAN JENNIFER MACLEAN JOHN MACLEAN JOHN E. MACLEAN KEITH MACLEAN NEIL MACLEAN RODERICK MACLEAN CAROLE ANNE MACLELLAN JOSEPH MACLELLAN MICHAEL G MACLENNAN ALLISTER MACLEOD ANGELA MACLEOD DOUGLAS MACLEOD ALEX J. MACNEIL BERNARD W. MACNEIL DANIEL PATRICK MACNEIL DONALD MACNEIL J. ALEXANDER MACNEIL JOHN MACNEIL KARLA A MACNEIL NORMAN MACNEIL RON MACNEILL TRACY MACNEILL RANDY K MACNUTT JOSLYN MACPHERSON WILLIAM MACPHERSON ALEXANDER MACQUARRIE ROBERT S MACTAGGART DANIEL MACZKO JIM MADDEN MICHAEL MADDOCKS HAZEL MADORE REX S. MADORE SUSAN MADSEN NORM MADSON BLAIR A MAGAS BRIAN W MAGEE LEONARD R. MAH HARRY D MAHARAJ KEVIN MAHONEY THOMAS MAHONEY CLEO MAJOR GEORGE MAJOR SIMON K. H. MAK BRYAN R. MAKEPEACE RICHARD MAKKINGA JOHN MALCOLM SHANE MALDEN JEAN MALETTE YASH P MALHOTRA MUKESH MALIK RAJESH MALIK DERRICK MALINOWSKI YVON MALLET J RAYMOND MALLEY SANDRA MALLEY WAYNE W MALLEY GEORGE MALOFE NICK MALYCHUK AMIN MANJI MUNIRA MANJI ANTHONY MANKOWSKI PAUL MANKOWSKI ROBERT H. MANN LYNN MANNING WILLIAM J MANNING PETER MANNISTU COLIN G MANSFIELD ANTHONY J MARCH KENNETH MARCH ALICE MARCHAND GARY C. MARCHANT GERALD W MARCHANT RHONDA MARCHANT HUGH A MARCHESI DEBRA MARDELL MARIO M MARINI DAVID MARK VERN MARKHAM WAYNE MARKLEY CAROLINE MARLOWE SYLVAIN MARQUIS JOHN MARRA CHRISTOPHER R. MARSH DAVID MARSHALL FRED MARSHALL PETER MARSHALL WILLIAM A MARSHALL DOUG MARTEL JULIA E. MARTEN LAWRENCE MARTEN RAYMOND MARTEN CYNTHIA A MARTIN JAMES MARTIN JOHN MARTIN KENNETH MARTIN MARGARET MARTIN MICHAEL J. MARTIN PAUL M MARTIN PIERRE L. MARTIN JR. THOMAS MARTIN TIMOTHY MARTIN TONY D. MARTIN DENISE MARTINEAU RANDY MARTINEAU ANNE MASCHING PAUL K MASCHING BEN J. MASK ALVIN J MASKWA RICHARD MASLANKO SHIRLEY MASLEN DOREEN MASON KEVIN MASON HADI MASRI WILLIAM MASSICOTTE MERLE MASTRACHUK ROBERT MATCHETT VICKI MATCHETT MARVEN A MATHESON ALEX MATHEW GERRARD E. MATHISON SATISH MATHUR DAVID E MATTHEWS CAROL MATTIE GARY J MATTIE LAURETTA MATTSON JAMES MAXWELL GERALD MAYNARD JOSEPH MAYNARD KEVIN T. MAYNER SHEILA MAYNER RON S. MAZEROLLE ANDREW MAZUR ANDY MAZUR STANLEY MAZURE AL J MCALLISTER JOHN J. MCATEER GLENN A. MCAULEY MURRAY MCAVOY DON MCBRIDE MICHAEL MCCAFFREY GARRY MCCAGG VINCENT MCCALLUM EDDIE MCCANN MARION MCCANN RAYMOND MCCANN WILLIAM MCCANN IAN MCCARTHY WILLIAM B MCCARTNEY KENNETH C. MCCLAIN EDGAR GORDON MCCLINTON DAVE MCCLURE ANDREW MCCOLL PHYLLIS MCCOMBE RICHARD MCCOMBE CLARENCE MCCONNELL CARL J MCCOY ELIZABETH K. MCCUE ROBERT MCCUE ANDREW J MCCULLOCH M DOUGLAS MCCULLOUGH GARRY A. MCCUMBER STEVE MCCUTCHEON BRIAN MCDONALD COLIN MCDONALD DORIS MCDONALD GEORGINA MCDONALD JAMES MCDONALD MARC MCDONALD MARILYN MCDONALD MARY MCDONALD MAUREEN MCDONALD MAURICE A. MCDONALD REGINALD MCDONALD ROGER MCDONALD SHEILA MCDONALD TEENA L. MCDONALD BRENT J MCDONELL J MCDOUGALL KENNETH D. MCDOUGALL LYLE J. MCDOUGALL STEVEN L MCDOUGALL KEVIN MCDOWELL JUDY MCFATRIDGE KEITH MCFATRIDGE JAMES MCGEE EDNA MCGEOUGH LARRY MCGHEE MARILYNN MCGIVERN SUZANNE MCGLADDERY PATRICK MCGLOIN EDWARD P. MCGRATH GERALD MCGRATH THOMAS J MCGREGOR DEAN MCINNIS DENNIS MCINNIS MAYNARD L. MCINNIS BROCK A. MCINTOSH DWIGHT MCINTOSH GREGORY MCINTOSH JOHN R MCINTOSH KEVIN N MCISAAC RHONDA MCISAAC DONALD G MCIVER ALAN MCKANE BRUCE W. MCKAY DAVID MCKAY JAMES MCKAY JAMES F MCKAY LYLE D MCKAY MARGARET MCKAY NORMAN MCKAY ROBERT MCKAY GEORGE MCKEAG DIANE MCKEE KERRY MCKEE WAYNE MCKEE GORDON T MCKENNA AARON L MCKENZIE BEVERLEY A MCKENZIE CALVIN MCKENZIE ELLA MCKENZIE ETHEL MCKENZIE JOSEPH MCKENZIE LYLENE J MCKENZIE PATRICK N MCKENZIE WARREN MCKENZIE WAYNE MCKENZIE PAUL C. MCKEOWN WAYNE MCKIM NEIL MCKINLEY JAMES MCKINNON BARRIE MCKITRICK CRAIG MCKNIGHT IAN MCLACHLAN LARRY MCLAUGHLIN BRIAN MCLEAN JACK C. MCLEAN NEIL MCLEAN MURRAY MCLELLAN PAT K MCLELLAN ROBERT MCLENNAN GARY MCLENNON DAVID MCLEOD DENNIS N. MCLEOD DWAYNE D MCLEOD JANET L. MCLEOD KIMBERLY MCLEOD NORMAN MCLEOD ROBERT G MCLEOD TOM J. MCLERNON JOSEPH MCMEECHAN JAMES R MCMILLAN STEVEN MCMILLAN BRUCE ROBERTSON MCMULLIN JAMES N. MCMULLIN MICHAEL MCMULLIN DANIEL MCMURDO RICHARD MCNALL SHELLEY MCNALL GLENN MCNALLY TERRANCE W. MCNALLY J. I. C. MCNAUGHTON DONALD S MCNEIL GORDON MCNEIL GARY MCNEILLY KARI MCNEILLY MICHAEL MCPHERSON GERALD E. MCPHILLAMEY PAUL B. MCQUAY S. MCQUITTY DONALD B. MCRAE JIM MCTURK ANDREW J. MCWILLIAM SHERRI MEARS VIRGINIA MEDLEYLANE JOHN F. MEEHAN KEVIN W. MEEK WALTER MEGLEY VINOD K. MEHTA CARLA MEIER DONALD MEIER KARL MEIER BONNIE MEIKLEJOHN RAYMOND MEINTS PIERRE MEKISH DERRICK D. MELANSON DAVID J MELDRUM ROGER E. MELLEY JOHN MELLON MICHAEL MELLON VIVIEN MELLON BARBARA MELNICHUK DAVID N. MELNICHUK LEONARD MELNICHUK SIDNEY L. MELONEY DANIEL MENARD ROLAND C. MENCHENTON GODWIN K MENSAH ANDREW MERCER DENIS MERCER DENNIS EDWARD MERCER EDWARD B. MERCER GILBERT MERCER GRAHAM C. MERCER RYBERN MERCER SHIRLEY MERCER LENA MERCREDI LORETTA MERCREDI LAURIE L MERRICK ROBERT MERRICK HELEN E MERSEREAU DONITA M.F. MESSENGER BURTON C. METCHEWAIS DARRYL METZ TED MEYERS ERNEST MICHAEL JOHN W. MICHAEL RICHARD MICHAEL ALLEN MICHALKO BRENDA MICHALKO LAURIER MICHAUD MARIO MICHAUD DAVID MICHELIN HAROLD MICHELIN ARNOLD J. MICHETTI STEPHEN MICK ROGER GM MICKALKO GARY MIDDLEBROOK ALEXANDER MIDDLETON CHRISTOPHER MIDFORD EDWARD MIERZEWSKI GORDON MIHOTICH ALBERT MILES ANN MILES GORDON MILES MICHAEL MILES HAROLD J. MILLAR HOLLY MILLAR PAUL E. MILLAR ANDREA MILLER ANDREW MILLER ARDEN A. MILLER BERNARD MILLER DAVID R MILLER ERIC MILLER GLEN E. MILLER IAN A. MILLER LAWRENCE MILLER LORRAINE MILLER PATRICIA MILLER EDWARD A MILLMAN BRIAN MILLS FRED MILLS WILLIAM MILLS DONALD MILNE GEORGE MILNE DESMOND MILNER WAYNE D. MIMURA DON MINARD LYDIA MINGO BRENDAN MINTER BRENT MITCHELL DAVID MITCHELL JAMES MITCHELL WAYNE B MITCHELL SCOTT MOAR JOHN B. MOFFAT MARILYN MOFFAT NORMAN J. MOFFAT ZAINOUL MOHAMED JOHN MOHAMMED DAVID L. MOIR LESLIE MOIR WILLIAM MOLLARD RAYMOND MOLLOY VINCENT MOLLOY MICHELLE MOLYNEUX GERARD V. MONAGHAN AGUEDA MONCHERRY GEORGE W A MONCHERRY OSCAR MONPLAISIR CLIFFORD J. MONTPETIT JOYCE MONTROY CHRIS MOONEY GERALD MOONEY KAREN MOONEY ANTHONY MOORE BRIAN MOORE BRIAN E. MOORE CALVIN MOORE DARREN MOORE FRANK MOORE GARRY A. MOORE RHONDA MOORE RUSSEL MOORE WAYNE MOORE BRENDA MOORES DANNY G. MOORES JUNE MOOTOO-REECE JEAN MOREAU BILL MORFITT VALERIE MORFITT DOUGLAS MORGAN HELEN MORGAN KERRY MORGAN KURT MORGAN MICHELE MORGAN PETER MORGAN RONALD L MORGAN WALTER J. MORIARTY ERNEST MORIN GAETAN P. MORIN MARC MORIN MICHEL RENE MORIN PAUL MORIN ADOLF MORITZ RICK MORLEY JOHN R. MORONEY MONICA D MORPHY BARRY R MORRELL GREG MORRELL CLYDE R. MORRIS JOHN BERNARD MORRIS BRUCE MORRISON DAVID L MORRISON GERALD MORRISON MURRAY MORRISON SHAWN MORRISON STEPHEN MORRISON WILLIAM R MORRISSEY GLEN MORROW ANTHONY MORT THOMAS A. MORTENSEN ROY MOSELEY LARRY A MOSENG BOYD MOSS IAN C. MOSS BOB MOTTERN ARCHIE MOUNTAIN MALCOLM MOUNTEER PETER MOUSEK BEULAH B. MOWAT KIRBY J. MOYSEY DARIN MUDGE EBERHARD MUELLER PAMELA D MUELLER RUDOLPH MUELLER DONNA MUHLBEIER BRIAN MUIR BRIAN MUIR DOUGLAS MUIR ERIC J MUISE FREDERICK MUISE AVINASH MUJOOMDAR PATRICK J. MULHALL CYRIL MULLALY DOROTHY MULLALY GARY J. MULLALY CHRISTOPHER T. MULLEN SEAN MULLEN WILLIAM MULLEN HERMAN MULLER MARK J MULLIN MIKE J. MULLIN ELAINE MULLINS GARY M MULLINS GERARD MULLINS WAYNE MULROONEY JAMES E. MUNCASTER ALISTAIR MUNDELL BRUCE MUNRO NORBERT MURAWKA IAN MURDOCH JAMES A. MURDOCH DAVE M MUROWCHUK CLIFF MURPHY DAN A. MURPHY DENNIS F. MURPHY MAUREEN MURPHY MELVIN MURPHY SEAN MURPHY TERENCE MURPHY TIMOTHY MURPHY WILLIAM MURPHY GRAEME A. MURRAY ROBERT MURRAY NICK MUSHEY SHIRLEY MUSHEY DANNY MUSSEAU TONY MUSWAGON WALID MUWAIS MARTIN MUZYKA GERRARD MYLES ISHMAEL O (TOM) MYLES JAMES MYLES JAMES A. NADASDI JARMILA NADEMLEJNSKY GEOFF P. NAGLE JOHN NAHAMKO BARRY NAMETH CHARLES F. NASH J. NASH PETER G. NASH PHYLLIS NASH RICHARD NASH THOMAS D NASH GURINDER NATT RICARDO E. NAVARRO NANCY NAVEN CHERKEWICK GARY NAYLER RONALD G. NEATBY JOHN NEEDHAM OWEN NEIMAN TARA NELSON DEBORAH NEMEY AMIR NENSI NIMROD N NERBAS MORRIS NESDOLE D NETTERVILLE J. KEN NEUFELD MARY NEUFELD JAMES NEVE FRANK NEVEU GLEN NEWBIGGING ERIC P. NEWELL JAMES F.A. NEWMAN JOHN M. NEWMAN FRED L. NEWTON SAMSON Y M NG RANDY NICHOLLE DARRELL M NICHOLS MARIE H. NICHOLS PAUL NICHOLS TERRY NICHOLS JEFFERY M. NICHOLSON DAVID NICKEL KENNETH R NICKERSON DR PETER NICKERSON DOUGLAS R NICOL RAYMOND W. NICOLLE JEAN NIELSEN WILLIAM A. NIELSEN MILOSLAV NIKL RICK NILSON PETER NILSSON JOYCE NISBET MARGARET A. NISBET KAREN NISH CHARLES D.C. NIXON LINDA NIXON RAYMOND NIXON RODNEY NIXON THERESA NIXON THOMAS A. NIXON MARILYN NOBLE MURRAY P. NOBLE S ROSS NOBLE RICHARD NODDER BYRON NOEL HUGH W. NOEL ROBERT A NOEL RITA NOH MARINA NOKOHOO DAN NOLAN SAMUEL NOLAN WILLIAM MAURICE NOLAN MARYANNE NONAY MIKE NOON SHAHAB H. NOORANI CLIFF NORBERG RANDY A. NORDICK MAUREEN NORDLI PEGGY NORDLUND ERIC R. NORDMAN CARL NORDQUIST KEVIN NORMAN LEWIS R. NORMAN LORNE K. NORMAN RANDY NORMAN ROBERT L. NORMAN RICHARD NORMANDEAU ALEXIS NORMORE ERIC D NORMORE SHAWN NORMORE ANNETTE NORONHA HAROLD R. NORTHCOTT LEWIS NORTHCOTT DOUGLAS H. NORTHEY MARLENE NORTHEY FREDERICK A NORTHUP CYRIL GREGORY K NOSEWORTHY REX NOSEWORTHY WILLIAM K. NOSEWORTHY BRENT WILLIAM NOVLESKY VINCENT J. NOWLAN RAYLENE NUGENT JOCELYNE NUTTALL ELMER D. NYKIFORUK JOAN NYKIFORUK PENNY A NYKIFORUK MILES B NYSTROM EDWARD B. O'BRIEN LORRAINE O'BRIEN MARILYN E. O'BRIEN P. EAMONN O'BRIEN PATRICK O'BRIEN SEAN O'CALLAGHAN DARREN O'CONNOR EAMONN O'CONNOR JOHN O'CONNOR JOHN P. O'CONNOR LOYOLA I O'CONNOR SHIRLEY O'CONNOR NEIL O'DONNELL RICHARD O'DONNELL KEVIN J. O'GORMAN RALPH O'GRADY DAVE O'HALLORAN CHARLES J. O'HANLEY CONOR J. O'LEARY PATRICK G. O'NEAL BLAIR O'NEILL PATRICK O'NEILL MICHAEL O'QUINN ROBERT OATES NOLA R OGAR KAREN OGILVY MICHAEL OHALLORAN GARRY W. OKE CAROL OLEKSOW BRUNO K. OLESEN VALERIE OLESEN MICHAEL J OLINECK OREST OLINECK HEATHER OLIVER MS DAVID OLIVER JOHN OLIVER JUDITH A OLIVER THOMAS W. OLIVER LARRY N. OLSEN CHARLES WAYNE OLSON RANDY OLSON MONICO OPRECIO ROBERT

L. ORCHARD CHARLENE ORCHESKI EUGENE ORCHESKI LYNN ORGAN BRUCE ORO BRAD ORR GARRY B OSBORN ADEMOLA OSENI CINDY OSMOND CLIFFORD OSMOND SCOTT E. OSMOND LIONEL OSTIGUY ANDREW OSTROWSKI THAD P. OSTROWSKI CAROL OUELLETTE GERALDINE OUILON NATALIE OUIMET GREGORY OUTHOUSE CAROLYN OVERHOLT MICHAEL P. OVERHOLT DONALD OVERLAND GERALD OVERMAN MARK OVERWATER R. JOHN OXENFORD ALLAN T PAANANEN LORNE PAANANEN WILLIAM PAANANEN WILLIAM WC PACEY EDWARD A PAGE JOHN P PAGE KAREN PAINE RANDALL PAINE M PALAHNIUK ALAN PALLETT LLOYD PALMER EDWARD PALSKY PORFIRIO PANGILINAN BRIAN W.G. PAPINEAU BERNARD PAQUETTE FRED W. PAQUETTE RANDY PARADIS EDWARD PARADOWSKI BEVERLY PARANYCH JEAN PARENT EWALD PARIDAEN JOHN R. PARK ANTHONY W PARKER DANIEL G PARKER IAN PARKER RON PARKER DEREK WILLIAM PARKES IAN PARKINSON JOHN B. PARKS SARAH PARKS HARJIVAN M PARMAR MARGARET E. PARNHAM RICHARD PARR SIMON PARR CARLOS PARRA BERNARD J. PARRELL GAYLE PARROTT GLENN D PARRY KAREL O.A. PARSCH BERNARD J. PARSLEY KELLY PARSLEY KEVIN F. PARSLEY RICHARD PARSON ALBERT S PARSONS BARRY PARSONS BENJAMIN PARSONS DANIEL PARSONS DEREK JOHN PARSONS DIANE PARSONS FRANK PARSONS GEORGE PARSONS GEORGE E. PARSONS GLEN PARSONS GUY PARSONS HAROLD PARSONS HEATHER PARSONS HILDA PARSONS IRVING PARSONS JAMES PARSONS JAMES W. PARSONS JERRY PARSONS KENNETH J. PARSONS LESLIE PARSONS RHODA I. PARSONS ROCKWELL PARSONS SHERRY PARSONS VALDA PARSONS W JOSEPH PARSONS WAYNE A. PARSONS WILLIAM PARSONS BETTY PARTRIDGE DONALD W. PARTRIDGE CORNELL C. PASICHNUK MARY PASKAL MICHAEL PASKAL DANIEL J PASTIRIK SHIRLEY PATENAUDE CLIFFORD G. PATON JOHN A PATON LAUREEN PATON TIMOTHY PATRICK DONELDA PATTERSON GORDON PATTERSON LEO PATTERSON PAUL PATTERSON TIM PATTERSON VERNON I PATTERSON MICHAEL J. PAUL DAVID PAULIN JEANETTE PAULS RONALD W. PAULS WIESLAW PAWLOWSKI CLAUDE PAYNE FREDERICK R. PAYNE GARY S. PAYNE HERMAN PAYNE PAUL PAYNE REGINA PAYNE ROBERT PAYNE TIM PAYNE CHARLENE PEAKE RANDY PEARCE ANGELA PEARSON ARTHUR T. PEARSON DELROY A. PEART DEREK PEATS INGRID P. PECK LAURENCE H. PECKFORD RALPH PECKFORD BYRON PEDDLE CLIFFORD PEDDLE GARY PEDDLE MAXWELL PEDDLE MAXWELL W. PEDDLE SHEILA PEDDLE STEPHEN J PEDDLE JACK H PEDEN GORDON PEDERSON LAURA PEDERSON WALTER D PEERS CHRISTOPHER J. PEFFERS EUGENE PELECH G PELLETIER GAETAN Y. PELLETIER MARC DENIS PELLETIER DONALD PELLEY WALTER PELTONEN THEODORE PEMBERTON RAYMOND A PENAFIEL SIXTO PENAFIEL CLAYTON R. PENNELL ROBIN PENNER DEREK PENNEY DIANE M. PENNEY DOUGLAS F PENNEY GERALD PENNEY ROSEMARY PENNEY WARRICK G. PENNEY WOODROW L. PENNEY CHARLES PENNY JOAN PENNY BARRY PEPIN GILLES O. PEPIN SHELLEY C. PEPPER MELVIN PERCHINSKY MICHAEL PERDUE LINDA PEREPELUK THOMAS PEREPELUK TIMOTHY PERIZZOLO RICHARD J. PERKS ROBERT GRAHAM PERKS DARRELL PERREAULT MARCIA PERREIRA ROBERT D. PERRIN DARREL B PERRON LUCIEN M PERRON ANTHONY P. PERRY DAVID PERRY STEVE PERRY SHEILA PERSAUD ROLAND PERU SHAUKAT PERVEZ WOLFGANG PETER ALBERT A PETERS ALFRED T PETERS GRAEME PETERS IAN WILSON PETERS ROCKY JOHN PETERS TERANI PETERS TERRY A. PETERS VINCENT PETERS CINDY L. PETERSON DAWNE H. PETERSON DONALD E G PETERSON SHARON PETERSON JAY PETIGARA CINDY PETIPAS PAUL PETIPAS TONY G. PETIPAS BRIAN H.J. PETITE WILLIAM S. PETLYK BARRY PETRUK RYAN PETRUK BYRON PFLUG RENE I. PHALEMPIN PAUL PHEE WILLIAM PHEE ARTHUR C PHIBBEN J.B.M. PHILBIN BOB PHILIPOW CECIL J. PHILLIPS DIANE M. PHILLIPS LANCELOT PHILLIPS ROBERT PHILLIPSON BRIAN PHILP RICHARD PICHE TONY PICHERT LEO PICIACCHIA DONNA PICKENS WILLIAM PICKENS CRAIG PICKETT GEORGE L. PICKETT JOANNE PICKETT RONALD PICKETT SEWARD PICKETT WAYNE PIEPGRASS ALAN W. PIERCE CLARENCE E PIERCEY GLENDA PIERCEY LEONARD G PIERCEY BOYSIE PIERRE GREGORY PIERRE JOEL E PIERSON PETER PIETRAMALA GARRY PIGEON CHARLES L. PILGRIM DAVID PILGRIM KIRBY PILGRIM BONNIE L. PILKEY WILLIAM K. PILLER FORD PINKSEN RANDY PINKSEN RAYMOND R.P. PINTO GORDON L PIPER MAXINE PITRE TERRY PITRE PAUL PIVARNYIK LAWRENCE E. PLACATKA ARMAND PLAMONDON BART G. PLAMONDON WADE PLAMONDON EDWARD G. PLANTE GARY PLANTE HOWARD V PLANTE RANDY PLANTE DAVID PLATT JOHN PLAYFORD GARY R. PLAYTER DAVID PLEWS MILAN PODSEDNIK CAROL POERSCH DANIEL N. POETSEMA DAVID W. POGUE ADRIEN A. POIRIER PIERRE E POIRIER ROBERT J. POIRIER ADRIAN POITRAS CLAUDE POITRAS DAVID POLEY KEVIN POLLITT TERRY POLLOCK WILLIAM D. POLLOCK GLENDON D. POND LLOYD W. POND ROBERT PONG RUDY PONGO MICHAEL PONGRACZ GARY POOL GLENN V. POPE ROBERT POPOWICH DEBBIE POPPE DOUGLAS W. POPPE ALFRED POPPEN HOLLY PORRITT STEPHEN F. PORTER DENNIS A. PORTH NANCEE POSTE JOHN POTKINS ROBERT A POTKINS DERRICK POTTS KEN POTTS WILLIAM K POULSON MARTIN POULTON LAWRENCE POWDER MICKEY POWDER NORMA MARIE POWDER PETER POWDER CAROL POWELL KJERSTI POWELL ROBERT (BOB) POWELL ROY POWELL TONY J. POWELL RICHARD W. POWELSON ALLYN T. POWER GEORGE FRANCIS POWER HEATHER POWER JAMES POWER JEROME M. POWER PATRICK F. POWER WANDA POWER J. CRAIG PRATT LEAH A. PRATT TIM L PRAUGHT BRUCE PREDHAM DARLENE PREDHAM MALCOLM PRENDERGAST PATRICIA PRENDERGAST BRAD A. PRENTICE KELVIN PRESAKARCHUK CLIFFORD PRETTY SCOTT PRETTY WAYNE PRETTY KEN PREVILLE JERRY W. PRICE JOSEPH B. PRICE ROBERT BRUCE PRICE PAULINE PRIMEAU SAVERIO PRIMIANI BERTIE R. PRINCE DOUG PRINCE ERVAN PRINCE PHIL PRINS LARRY PRITCHETT LARRY P. PROCINSKY BRIAN PROCTOR VALDON PRODANIUK DONALD PROVENCAL RAYMOND C. PROVENCAL ROBERT E. PRUDEN JAN PRUS-CZARNECKI DR GREG PSUTKA CYRIL J. PUGH TONY B. PUHALSKI JANET PUHALSKIE STANLEY J. PUHALSKIE FREDERICK PUI MARTIN C. PULFER ROGER PUN ALCIDE DEAN PUNKO THOMAS PURCELL BRUCE P PURCHASE ROD PURCHASE DAVID PURVIS SHEILA PURVIS RICHARD N. PUTTOCK ROSE A. PYKE ERNE CHARLES PYLE DONALD EDGAR QUAPP MICHAEL QUARSHIE EDWARD J. QUEREL DAVID QUIGLEY HUGH QUIGLEY SALLY QUIGLEY LORNE A. QUINN MICHAEL QUINN ERNEST A. QUINTON SCOTT C. QUINTON MARILEE QUIST RICHARD N. QUIST EDWARDO QUITO OFELIA QUITO GEOFFREY RACKETTE HOWARD RADFORD JIM RADKE JAMES RAFFERTY JAVED IQBAL RAJA JOSEPH RAJHARD PAT RAJHARD IAN RALLON RONALD RALLON CARL RALPH PERRY RALPH VERNON RALPH RALPH RAMCHANDAR KHAMRAJIA RAMNATH POORAN RAMNATH ROOKMIN RAMNATH RONALD RAMSARAN D. ROLAND RAMSAY TONY RANDELL RAYMOND A RANGER STANLEY G. RAPP MARIENNE RAWLINGS LEON E RAY ROLAND RAYMOND JOHN L. RAYNARD PETER C READ TERRENCE READMAN PETER REAVILL D. REBBETOY BARRY JOHN REDDING JOHN C. H. REDDING DORIS REDDINGTON BARRIE REDERBURG CHRISTOPHER A. REDFEARN GORDON REED LYLE K REED ALWYN REES CORALIE REES DOUGLAS REES JOAN REES THOMAS W. REES DARYL REESOR JOHN REEVES BRUCE REGENSBURG RON A. REGUSH ALLAN L. REICH KENNETH J. REICHSTEIN BARRY REID CALVIN REID CANNIS REID CORBETT H. REID DALTON REID DAMIEN REID DEBBIE REID E. LEE REID EDWARD REID JACK REID JAMES REID JEFF REID LOUIS JOHN REID MARLENE G REID ROBERT REID RONALD J. REID DONNA REILEY RICHARD REIS ROLAND REMILLARD JOHN G. RENNIE SELINA RENO DELLAS W. RENTON LARRY RENTON LLOYD H. RENTON MURRAY M. RENTON SHELLEY A. RENTON GUIDO M. REPATO GEORGE REPCHUK GILLES REQUIER GUY V.R. REQUIER COLLEEN RESTOULE GUILLERMO RETAMALES TIM REVEGA BRADLEY REYNOLDS DAVID A. REYNOLDS HECTOR G REYNOLDS RON REZEWSKI JOHN RHIND ROBERT A RHIND JATINDER S RIAT CANDACE RICE GLENN RICE TONY RICE CHARLES RICHARD COLIN C RICHARDS FRANCIS R. RICHARDS GEORGE C. RICHARDS SEAN RICHARDS ALAN D. RICHARDSON EILEEN RICHARDSON KENNETH J. RICHARDSON RONALD RICHARDSON DIANE C. RICHER THOMAS RICKER DALE RIDEOUT WINSTON E. RIDEOUT JOHN M RIDLEY ANDREW RIEGLER JAMES RIGGS WALTER C. RILKOFF LESTER RIMMER LISA RIMMER PAUL RIMMER CHRISTOPHER H. RINGSTAD MARGARET E. RINTOUL LEONARD J RIOUX TIM RIOUX WILHELMINA RIP PAUL M. RIPCO ERNIE RIPKA ROBERT RIPLEY GREGORY A. RITCH DEBORAH E RITZ DON RITZ JAMES H. ROBBINS PAT ROBBINS BLAIR ROBERTS BOB M. ROBERTS DORELLE ROBERTS FAITH ROBERTS JACK ROBERTS JEFFREY ROBERTS ORVAN ROBERTS DONALD ROBERTSON WAYNE D. ROBERTSON JEFFREY A ROBERTSSON DANIEL B. ROBICHAUD NORMAN ROBIDOUX MICHAEL G. ROBILLARD CLIVE D. ROBINS BARRY ROBINSON KENNETH ROBINSON MARYANN ROBINSON MURIEL E ROBINSON ROBERT J. ROBINSON PERRY ROBITAILLE MELVIN ROBLEE ROBERT G ROBOTHAM CHARLES F. ROCKWELL ROSS RODGERS A. BAYANI G. RODRIGUEZ ANTONIO R. RODRIGUEZ DINNA RODRIGUEZ BRUCE ROGERS CALVIN S ROGERS DERM ROGERS EDWARD ROGERS JAMES ROGERS MICHAEL ROGERS MICHAEL E. ROGERS ROBERT ROGERS BLAINE ROLLING GREGORY G ROMANISZYN WALTER ROMANIUK MARLENE RONNENBERG WILLIAM G. RONNENBERG KENNETH ROPCEAN PATRICIA ROPER NORBERTO G. ROSAL IRVIN F. ROSE D. GRANT ROSS DENZIL V. ROSS KENNETH ROSS ROBERT C. ROSS KIM ROSSELL BYRON ROSSER JOHN ROSTICKI DORIS ROTH NONNIE ROTH SAMUEL ROTH THEODORE ROTH THOMAS ROURKE DENIS ROUTHIER GLEN W ROVANG D. HENRY ROWBOTTOM DAVID J. ROWE GEORGE ROWE GEORGE F. ROWE RICHARD ROWE BOYDE ROWSELL BARBARA ROWSON BRIAN ROY CATHY J ROY CLIFFORD ROY MYLES ROY RANDOLPH K RUBY MERLE R. RUDIAK ROBERT RUDIGER DELORES RULE BOYD C. RUMBALL GILBERT E. RUMBOLT SHERRY RUNDLE DONNA RUSNAK COLIN B RUSSELL HILLARY RUSSELL JACK RUSSELL L. JOHN RUSSELL RAYMOND J. RUSSELL W. PATRICK RUSSELL NEIL E. RUTLEY BILL RYAN BRENDAN C. RYAN FRANCIS J. RYAN GERALD RYAN HUBERT C RYAN JOHN P. RYAN MARILYN D. RYAN MELVIN RYAN MICHAEL RYAN PATRICK S. RYAN WAYNE D. RYAN JOHN RYRIE RICHARD SAARI HOWARD H SABINE MARGARET SABINE CLYDE SACREY LESLIE F. SACREY PLEMAN SACREY DON J. SAINDON YVETTE SALE DON SALIBA HEBER W. SALLENBACH DAN SALOMONS SAM SALTER ROBERT M. SALYZYN NICHOLAS D. SALZL SHANI SAMARASINGHE DARREN SAMMANN GORDON SAMPSON GORDON E SAMPSON LORI-ANNE M SAMPSON LOWELL A. SAMS EASOW SAMUEL CHRISTOPHER SAND GERALD H. W. SANDERS JOHN SANDERSON RAIMONDO SANFILIPPO DR EMERSON C. SANFORD CARLTON R. SANSOM HARI SHANKER SARASWAT SUKHAMOY SARKAR NEIL HARVEY SASS ALBERT SAUCIER GERRY SAULNIER JEANNIE S. SAULNIER DESMOND SAUNDERS ELWOOD SAUNDERS FRED S. SAUNDERS HARRY SAUNDERS KENNETH E. SAUNDERS KEVIN SAUNDERSON ROLLIE SAUVE WILLIAM F. SAVANT PIERRE P SAVARD ALEXANDER SAWERS BEBI SAWH MOHAN SAWH DORIS J SAXTON PAUL SCANLON PHILLIP G. SCARLETT WILLIAM C. SCEVIOUR LYLE M. SCHAITEL DARRELL SCHEERS TOM SCHEURWATER ALDOLF F SCHEYBELER BRUCE M SCHIEWE WAYNE D. SCHIEWE RANDOLPH L. SCHLENDER TRACY SCHLOENDORF DAVID SCHMIDT FRED R. SCHMIDT ROBERT D SCHMIDT ROBERT F SCHMIDT BETTY SCHMULAND CHRIS SCHMULAND DELBERT L SCHMULAND GORDON P SCHMULAND CURTIS H. SCHNEIDER ERLE E. SCHOFIELD FELIX SCHRODER CHRISTIAN SCHROETER ALAN SCHUHMANN DONALD D. SCHULTE FRANK J. SCHULTE CARL H SCHULTZ LAURA SCHULTZ ROY SCHULTZ REINHARD.A (RON) SCHULZ BLAIR A SCHURMAN ROBERT SCHUTTE ALAN SCOTT BERTRAM L. SCOTT DAVID M. SCOTT GRAHAME P. SCOTT H SCOTT MICHELLE SCOTT RAYMOND SCOTT RICHARD SCOTT ROBERT SCOTT ROBERT T. SCOTT WILLIAM P SCOTT BILL SCRIVENER GEORGE W. SCRIVENER JOHN SCULLION IAN SCULLY VINCE SCULLY GERALD H SEAMAN MARILYN SEAMAN R.E. SEAMAN PAMELA SEARS JAMES A. SEATON GERRY E. SEATTER FRANK SEAWARD RICHARD SEEKINS HANIFA SEENANDAN KEIRON SEENANDAN RAJINDER SEHDEV ASHOK SEHGAL MANFRED SEIDL SUSAN SEIFFERT ANITA SEMPLE WALTER H. SENFT CAROLYN SENGER HAROLD I. SENGER DENNIS W. SENNETT DEBORAH SEREDA KARL D. SEREDA RICHARD A SERROUL ROB SERSON WENDY SERSON BRUCE SETTER CHARLENE SETTER KATHY SETTER MIKE SETTER LOURDES SEVERO BRIAN K. SEVERSON MARGARET SEVERSON RONALD C. SEVERSON CORNELIUS SEYTS GARY J SEYTS KENNETH SHAFFER CHANDRA J SHAH AJAY SHARMA DILIP K SHARMA VIR V. SHARMA JOHN SHARPE DOREEN SHARRON HAROLD P SHAVE JAMES D SHAVE RICHARD D. SHAW ROBERT C. SHAW WILLIAM H. SHAW LEO SHEA LORNE J SHEARING BARBARA SHEARS THOMAS M SHEARS TOM SHEARS ERNEST SHEAVES NORMAND SHEEHY SHELLEY SHEHINSKI WILLIAM E SHELFANTOOK GORDON C. SHELSWELL JOHN SHEPHERD FREEMAN A. SHEPPARD KEVIN SHEPPARD MELVIN D. SHERLOCK C SHERMAN C MARK SHERMAN DON CHARLES SHERMAN ROBERT SHERMAN KAREN SHERWIN GORDON SHEWCHUK RICHARD SHEWCHUK ELIZABETH H SHIELDS HSIU (SUE) SHIH PETER SHIH IGOR SHILIAEV BRIAN W. SHIMMONS HENRY SHIRT BONNIE SHORT JAMES J. SHORT JOHN F. SHORT WILLIAM B SHORT WILLIAM SHORT FENDY SHORTT WAYNE SHORTT DENNIS J. SHOTT HENRY SHOTT GORDON R. SHUGG BARBARA A. SHUMSKY KARL SHUSHKOVSKY DARREN SHYSH PETER SHYSH ANWAR SIDDIQI HARJOGINDER SIDHU EINNAR J SIGURDUR RICHARD C SILLANPAA MIKE J SILLARS JR DIANNE SILLARS MALCOLM J. SILLARS RONALD JOHN SIMAN BRENDA SIMCOE DAVID SIMCOE JOHN C. SIMMONDS WILLIAM H. SIMMONS ERNEST SIMMS FRANCIS SIMMS DENNIS SIMON HAROLD SIMON MILLAGE J. SIMON CAROLINE S SIMONS DANIEL L. SIMPSON DONALD SIMPSON JAMES SIMPSON RODWAY GEORGE SIMPSON DANIEL SINCLAIR JOE SINCLAIR JOHN W. SINCLAIR EDWARD SINGER SR GLORIA SINGER KEITH SINGER GURMUKH (GARY) SINGH VIRJANAND SINGH DEEPAK SINHA HARVEY SINNICKS WAYNE SINYARD ANN L. SITKO VIT M. SIUDA THAMBIMUTTOO SIVAGNANAM ROBERT SIY HAL M. SKAAR CLIFF SKEATES BERNARD SKINNER ROBERT SKWAROK W. KEITH SLADE JOHN A. SLAGHT DAVEY R. SLENO DAVID SLIZIAK WILLIAM SLOBODA CECILE SMALL PHILIP G SMALL RON SMALL THOMAS A. SMALLPIECE JOHN G. SMAR BRIAN R. SMART CLIVE G SMAR MURRAY SMART ALONZO W SMITH BARBARA SMITH BARRY G. SMITH BRETON J SMITH BURDEN R SMITH CHARLES E. SMITH CLARENCE SMITH DONALD SMITH EVELYN SMITH FLOYD D SMITH GARY SMITH GERALD SMITH GERALD SMITH GERRY E. SMITH HARLEY E. SMITH HARRY SMITH HERBERT SMITH HOWARD SMITH JAMES B. SMITH JOHN M SMITH LAURA SMITH LYNN SMITH MAXWELL SMITH MILTON A. SMITH ROBERT W SMITH ROBERT W SMITH RONALD SMITH RUSSELL G. SMITH SHARON SMITH STEPHEN SMITH SUSAN A. SMITH TERRENCE SMITH THOMAS E SMITH TODD SMITH TYLO SMITH VICKI L SMITH VICTOR G. SMITH WALLACE SMITH WILLIAM SMITH WILLIAM C SMITH BERNARD SMYTH MIKE SNEATH BRANT SNEDDON DAWN L. SNEDDON TODD SNEDDON ALLAN SNOOK BENJAMIN R. SNOOK BRIAN SNOOK DENISE SNOOK GERALD A. SNOOK ANNETTE SNOW ANTHONY SNOW CHRIS SNOW JOHN C SOBKOWICZ JUDY SOBOLEWSKI GURMEET SINGH SODHI SUSAN SOKORINSKI MERVIN SOKUL F JAVIER SOLA TREVOR M. SOLBAK LORNE SOLES ALLAN SOMERS LARRY SOMERVILLE IAN SOMMERVILLE WAYNE D SOOLEY CRAYTON SORENSEN WILLIAM SOUTH BRIAN J SOUVIE CHARLES SPACKMAN CLINTON SPACKMAN CHRIS SPADY MERV SPADY LIONEL SPAK MEL SPALLER JAMES SPANIER KELLY SPANIER BERNICE E. C. SPARKES DAVID SPARKES PATRICK SPARROW JONATHAN R SPENCE PAT J. D. M. SPENCE EDWARD SPENCE ROBERT G. SPENCER STEPHEN SPENCER LINDA SPENCLEY DEREK J SPICE NIGEL SPINK GREGORY SPOHN LARRY M. SPOHN JAMES SPOONEMORE HARVEY V. SPRING MURRAY SPRIN